YOU HEARD IT THROUGH THE GRAPEVINE

Stuart Walton is the author of *The World Encyclopedia of Wine, The Complete Guide to Wine, Wines of the World* and *Out of It: a Cultural History of Intoxication.* He has been wine writer for the *Observer, BBC Good Food* Magazine and *Food and Travel.* He lives in Brighton.

YOU HEARD IT THROUGH

THE GRAPEVINE

shattering the myths about the wine business

Stuart Walton

AURUM PRESS

First published in Great Britain
2001 by Aurum Press Ltd
25 Bedford Avenue, London WC1B 3AT

A catalogue record for this book is available from the British Library.

ISBN 1 85410 653 8

1 3 5 7 9 10 8 6 4 2
2001 2003 2005 2004 2002

Typeset in 11/17pt Perpetua by M Rules
Design by Roger Hammond
Index by Madeline Weston
Printed in Great Britain by MPG Books Ltd, Bodmin

for NWG

The best use of bad wine is to drive out poor relations.

— FRENCH PROVERB

'I rather like bad wine,' said Mr Mountchesney; 'one gets so bored with good wine.'

— BENJAMIN DISRAELI, SYBIL

Contents

preface

I NEVER USED TO DRINK wine. At least, I drank it when it was there, as it always was at student parties in Manchester, but it wasn't my top tipple. A couple of bottles of Liebfraumilch would get you well set-up for an evening's dancing and schmoozing and lacerating emotional breakdown, but I had no interest in wine as a special subject.

When I was in my early twenties – the age when other boys were moving on to their second cars and thinking about settling down – my parents bought me a glass cocktail-shaker for Christmas. As my friends and I filled it up time and again on Friday nights with blue drinks and pink drinks and drinks that nobody has ever drunk before or since, the permafrost landscape of the early-eighties recession drifted agreeably out of focus. In a state of flushed confusion one night we dropped and smashed the shaker, but my parents soon bought me another, this time an unbreakable one with my initials monogrammed on the side.

The cocktail era couldn't go on forever, though. Soon I was at Oxford, writing an M.Litt. thesis on Samuel Beckett under the great Terry Eagleton, and it was time to put such diversions aside.

Attending a meeting of a debating society at my college one evening, I was passed a bottle of twenty-year-old vintage port from the college's cellars, and another diversion came into my life. This tasted nothing like the sort of ruby cough-medicine I'd previously known as port, on which I had been weaned at the age of six weeks, when my mother had thoughtfully soaked my pacifier in it.

Back home up north, safely back in the bosom of the family and embarking on a misery year of unemployment, I began to watch a new BBC2 show called *Food and Drink*, on which – as part of an end-of-term Christmas special – Oz Clarke and Jilly Goolden played an entertaining game. They handed each other anonymous glasses of wine, each challenging the other to guess what they were. As they pinpointed the wines geographically the audience applauded, and I found myself thinking, 'What a top trick!'

A friend and I decided to try it at home. The first wine I was presented with was a thin, light white with a trace of lemon scent on it, but no other discernible personality. 'Italy?' I ventured, and my colleague gasped in disbelief. In London the following year to seek my fortune, I enrolled on the external wine course at Leith's School of Food and Wine, and came out of the final exam with 95.5%. Somewhat unexpectedly, I had discovered something else I could do.

These were the 1980s, and wine was then an exciting thing to be associated with. The weekend newspapers all had wine columns, and I took out a postal subscription to *WINE* magazine. In the summer of 1991, I wrote to Paul Levy, then food and wine editor of the *Observer*, and asked if he needed anyone to open bottles for the tastings. Mr Levy was rather short-handed all round, and I soon found myself doing a lot more than opening bottles. It was here, single-handedly uncorking 75 explosively lively sparkling wines for a marathon tasting, drenched in spurting fizz on a sunny Tuesday morning on yet another unauthorised skive from my day-job, that I became happily convinced my next career was being launched.

As the 1990s progressed, I did the whole wine writer's thing – the press trips, the tastings, the examinations, the stints as a wine columnist here, there and everywhere (including a short spell as wine writer on the *Observer* itself), and eventually the big, glossy, coffee-table book on wine that we all feel compelled to write. The night I arrived in Santiago de Chile on the press-trip circuit, ostensibly a veteran but actually a total virgin, I was filled with a palpable sense that I had at last found my best vocation.

I want to say that it was a great time to live through wine, but increasingly I was unable to shake off a feeling that not everything in the global vineyard is lovely. This book is the product of that creeping sense of unease. I now believe that all aspects of wine, from the way it is made to the way it is marketed to the way it is talked about, are infected to a dismaying degree with dishonesty and pretentiousness, and that there exists a kind of silent conspiracy to prevent the truth of this becoming known.

This isn't idol-smashing for the good old rowdy sake of it. There are still brilliant, memorable, extraordinary wines being made all over the globe, but there is an awful lot of ditchwater-dullness too, and our high-street retailers are buying it by the tanker-load and charging us £4.99 a bottle for it. Or £14.99 if it has bubbles. In this, they have been enthusiastically aided and abetted in recent years by writers happy to forsake any sense of editorial independence to take corporate money for promoting it. This has led to a vicious circle in which wine is becoming more and more monotonous, while the people who should be pointing this out can't be relied on to do so without getting stuck waist-deep in conflicts of interest.

Whether they'll ever let me drink wine in this town again after this, I don't know, but I feel the time has come to start spilling the beans. My aim is not to induce despair, or to drive you to drink that isn't good for you. You're still better off with wine than industrial vodka or bulk-produced lager. But if you care about the quality of what you drink, and even remember a time not so long ago when it was indisputably better than this, here are a few issues you might like to ponder. And if they ask you in the off-licence where you got all this, tell them you heard it through the grapevine . . .

I want to thank Paul Levy properly once and for all for lighting the blue touch-paper. It might just have happened in some other way without him, but I'm sure it wouldn't have been half so much fun or started my press career off at the top, which is my very favourite place to start anything. The International Wine Challenge, run by *WINE* magazine, is the best annual tasting opportunity in London and a credit to its organisers, and was a privilege to be part of for the several years they couldn't keep me away. Sue Harris is one of the more understanding and professional PR principals in the business, and may just forgive me once more for telling the tale about that unforgettable press trip to Chile.

At Aurum Press, Graham Coster has been an exemplary editor. I didn't detect a single tut as I fell haplessly behind my deadlines with an overloaded plate in the summer of 2000, and his interventions in the text have been timely, helpful and invariably worked to improve the finished article. As always, the support and ministrations of my literary agent Antony Harwood must be acknowledged. Without him, I would long since have been stuck somewhere much duller. And for the assistance of my tasting team – Nicholas, Tim, Brian, Clive and Tracey, Chris, Lewis, Roger and Dee – I am eternally, lovingly grateful.

Thank you again also to my parents, whose unwavering belief in me is beyond price, whether it's cocktail-shakers or Comtes de Champagne.

Stuart Walton

Brighton, November 2000

Chapter 1

A SURFEIT OF CHARDONNAYS

Or: How the brave new world of wine was won and lost

THERE'S A STATEMENT YOU MAY have read a number of times in the columns of wine writers or the price lists of retailers, that has now reached the status of an eternal verity. It goes: 'There has never been as much good wine on sale in Britain as there is today.' It's a claim we've all made from time to time, even those of us whose memories of wine retailing don't stretch back much further than the early 1980s. We have struggled through the dark ages of snobbery and elitism and emerged on to the sunlit uplands, where we romp and play among wines from all over the known world, revelling in the teeming variety and the infinite expansiveness of sheer, happy choice. If only . . .

There *was* a period when there was more good wine on sale in Britain than there is today. It was between ten and fifteen years ago when our palates were young and adventurous, the economy was enjoying an artificial boom, and serious wine was an integral accessory to the smartest new lifestyles. The high-street retailers moved swiftly and boldly to answer the demand with wines from the classic regions of Europe. There was *cru classé* Bordeaux on every supermarket shelf, there were QmP Rieslings from Germany and extraordinary offerings from the lesser-known corners of Italy, Spain and Portugal. There were enterprising wines from outside Europe too, from that sprawling exterior Eden that European flat-earthers were content to call the New World. You could even – *mirabile dictu* – buy wines from Alsace in Marks & Spencer.

Today, the scope of what the high-street outlets sell is considerably more restricted and timid. There is a slew of wines from Australia and Chile, the great majority Chardonnay, Cabernet Sauvignon and Merlot either singly or permutated, and Shiraz. There isn't much else from the rest of the Americas, or from New Zealand. Eastern Europe is much enhanced, the old Bulgarian reds joined now by varietals from Hungary and Romania. By contrast, the premier regions of France are much reduced, with bog-standard Bordeaux and Burgundy leading the charge, supported by oceans of varietal vin de pays d'Oc. There is always Muscadet, thin tasteless little Muscadet, although nobody remembers why. Of the huge diversity of the Rhône, the central Loire and Alsace, there is next to nothing. Nobody seems to venture very far into Gascony or Provence, where there are all sorts of interesting wines and indigenous grape varieties waiting to be discovered. Retailers happy to list three types of Chianti don't appear to take any interest in anywhere south of Tuscany, the pain in Spain falls mainly on Rioja, and

Portugal's newer regions, such as the Alentejo, Ribatejo and Terras do Sado are largely neglected, despite great improvements in wine-making technology there. Examples of serious German wine, as distinct from Liebfraumilch and Piesporter Michelsberg, are the double-yolked eggs of the wine trade.

How did this happen?

The economic collapse of the early 1990s had a lot to do with it, of course. In the eighties Sainsbury's had sold Jurançon, a gorgeously scented white wine from the south-west corner of France, M&S had an example of one of the rare white wines of Beaujolais, and Morrisons, the northern supermarket chain, offered its customers an *embarras de richesse* of five-star wine at the company's famously competitive prices. Riffling through one of the annually updated wine guides back then, you might have been tempted by the descriptions of Barbaresco or Savennières, and wouldn't have had to wander too long among the shelves of the off-licence chains and supermarkets to find one.

The recession killed all this stone-dead. As people drew in their financial horns, the daily or weekly purchase of wine was a prime area for savings, and as the less badly affected traded down in their choices, those who were really feeling the pinch cut wine out altogether. Restaurants emptied, the retail chains began closing branches, and the Gulf War of 1990 cast a pall over both business confidence and people's willingness to party. All sorts of industries went down the chute. Anybody who had set themselves up in business with the word 'consultant' printed on their cards soon woke up to a world in which there was no longer a ready market for telling people what to do. There were the image consultants who had advised companies on what kind of coffee to buy for visiting executives; the design consultants who had reconfigured everything from the letterhead to the colour of the seats in reception; the lifestyle consultants who had drawn up a jogging programme for the managing director and advised on best time-management strategies. There were also wine consultants who, at a commercial level, had attended wholesalers' trade tastings on behalf of restaurants and bars, in order to advise on the best wines to buy, and then write the wine list for them. In the private domain, they recommended the wisest wines to buy as a financial investment, or even simply a suitable bottle or two to accompany a dinner party menu. Before I got into the writing racket I even did a little of this myself. An ambulance service social club paid me £75 to choose better wines than they were already buying from the national wholesaler they had a contract with. When I first began helping to organise wine tastings at the *Observer* in 1991, it was as 'wine consultant' that I styled myself in the write-ups. In fact, the bottom had already dropped out of that market, and the consensus was that building up that majestic edifice again would probably take another twenty years.

That there had been a market at all for wine consultancy was reflected in the glorious diversity of what was on offer in the off-trade. In the late 1980s it was possible to walk into Marks & Spencer – admittedly the company's flagship Marble Arch branch – and be faced with the exquisite dilemma of whether to risk £15 on a 20-year-old *cru classé* Graves red from a dubious vintage. (I did, and it was as disappointing as the *Webster's Wine Guide* said it would be, but the fact that it was there at all gave an indication of how adventurously the company assumed its customers might buy.) The market for classed-growth clarets has now largely been ceded back to the specialist independent wine merchants where it had anyway traditionally resided, and the wines of Bordeaux are now most visibly represented in the high-street multiples in the form of horrendous branded wines, of which more in Chapter 3. In 1988 the job of a wine consultant would have been to warn people away from that superannuated Graves, and on to something further along the shelf. As the new century dawns, their job, it would seem – assuming anybody would do something as silly as employ a *soi-disant* wine consultant – would include advising the high-street buyer to avoid Bordeaux altogether.

As the consultants were swept aside in the cold blast of economic privation, the wine retailers hacked their buying back to the bone. As just one example, Majestic Wine, whose warehouses up and down the country made shopping for wine nothing less than a voyage of discovery, and who single-handedly bought wholesale by-the-case wine buying to the general public, became a flaccid imitation of itself virtually overnight. Previously its range had boasted a thrilling heterogeneity, running the gamut from ultra-fine burgundies and classed-growth clarets to recherché items such as Lebanese Château Musar and Valpolicella Amarone (the hugely alcoholic speciality version of that north-east Italian red, made from raisined grapes fermented all the way to bone-dry – an almost intimidatingly powerful wine with an aftertaste as bitter as lifelong regret). In the austerity that followed, when the slow movers had been cleared off the shelves, what was left was a lowest-common-denominator selection of everyday wines no more attractive than that being sold in the ordinary chains. Majestic's list has, in the last few years, come right back into contention, and the company even sells Amarone once more, but to say it got its fingers burned by the recession is an understatement – the recession altered its entire character as a wine merchant to an extent that the supermarkets, with their vast buying power, managed to escape.

However much their superstore branches have diversified into niche marketing of premium products, ready meals and so forth, the supermarkets' core business is still the teabags-and-tins they originally took over from the old corner shop, and to some extent they were able to ride out the recession when it came to wine. They simply cut out the more expensive varieties, the smaller parcels of speciality bottles, and concentrated attention on the everyday quaffing stuff that had always been the bulwark of their operations. These are the wines the supermarkets are curiously coy about displaying at the twice-yearly tastings they hold for the wine press. It is still possible to buy bottles of generic hock and low-alcohol Lambrusco in all the major chains at substantially less than £2 a bottle, although members of the wine-writing freemasonry could be forgiven for ignorance of the fact. Nonetheless, this is what kept the wine departments just about buoyant when everybody lost their sense of adventure. Better times having returned, we might have expected the hock to have gone the way of all Beaujolais Nouveau, but no, there it is still, peeping sheepishly out from between the Gallo Chardonnay and the Merlot vin de pays, bedded well in against the next economic maelstrom.

One has to maintain a sense of perspective, of course. No business, however large and powerful, can be faulted for adapting to adverse circumstances. However, the sense of evangelism brought to wine retailing in the 1980s has been lost, and looks unlikely to stage any sort of comeback in the near future. There is an unfathomable air of defeatism about this, especially when compared to other sectors of the supermarket trade. All the chains, for example, have latterly gone heavily into organic produce. Initially, the showing was limited to a couple of knobbly-looking pears and the odd filthy carrot at twice the price of the pesticide-coated specimens, but now the cost differential has eased, and there is organic pasta, cheese, rice, even organic microwaveable lasagne (and even the fruit has, enigmatically, become less knobbly). Having tapped into a certain modest level of consumer interest, the supermarkets have succeeded in augmenting their turnover from organic produce by offering products customers may never have been aware of needing. In this way the multiples have gladly taken on the role of market-makers.

Oddly, though, they have largely surrendered this role when it comes to wine. No longer do they seem interested in persuading customers to try new and unfamiliar appellations. They are only concerned with selling new and unfamiliar brands of Chardonnay alongside the Jacob's Creek. It's as if the experimentation of the eighties showed conclusively that what people wanted was the ever-same range of varietals. They had tried Bairrada *garrafeira*, and they preferred varietal Merlot. They had tried Alsace Pinot Gris, but what they liked was oaky Chardonnay. This is how the supermarket buyers read the runes, and with those ubiquitous wines their customers are now being force-fed.

There is about all this, to be sure, a certain sense of chicken-and-egg. Which comes first – the retailer's refusal to stock a certain type of wine, or the consumer's refusal to buy it? The wines of

Alsace are a useful case in point. It is a universal given of the wine trade that you cannot sell Alsace wine. Among the reasons for this are that the north-east corner of France is not a notably popular destination for British tourists; that the wines – although varietally labelled – are held to be too obscure for mainstream tastes (who knows what Pinot Blanc is supposed to taste like, let alone Sylvaner?); and that unacquainted customers think either that the wines are German, or that they will at least taste like German wines. The tall flute bottles look German; most of the grape varieties seem to be German – Riesling most of all; and the producers' names and the names of the individual vineyards, where cited, all sound German. Those who consider themselves too sophisticated for German wines therefore don't want them, while the hock and Liebfraumilch constituency will turn as pale as their favourite slosh at the prices. Other than by acts of aggression, of course, Alsace has not been German since the seventeenth century, and has not been German at all since it was snatched back from Hitler by French and American troops towards the end of the war. Notwithstanding this, Alsace wines are routinely confused with German wines. After Marks & Spencer had de-listed their two Alsace wines, a Gewurztraminer and a Pinot Gris (good ones too, from the co-operative at Pfaffenheim), I asked their senior wine buyer why they had bailed out of the region. 'Simple,' was his reply. 'We couldn't sell them.' Even less Alsace wine will be sold if it doesn't even appear on the shelves.

With other retailers the situation is much the same. Where Alsace wines are listed at all, they are nearly all from the Turckheim co-operative. Turckheim's are perfectly serviceable wines, even if the labels are irredeemably drab, but to be offered them every which way you turn constitutes a dreary failure of initiative on the part of the retailers. Even Oddbins, so innovative in many other respects, scarcely exerts itself in Alsace. Tasting a flight of gloriously aromatic, concentrated wines from the likes (as it turned out) of Hugel and Zind-Humbrecht at the International Wine Challenge several years ago, I was astonished to hear one major wine buyer declare, without elaboration, that he simply didn't like Alsace wine. A while back the Thresher chain attempted to steal a march on its main high-street rival Oddbins by buying a massive parcel of Alsace wines, even hiring Marco Pierre White to feed the journalists who came to the tasting, but their range has now shrunk back to Turckheim and a handful of Zind-Humbrecht, most of the latter only available at their more upmarket Wine Rack and Bottoms Up shops. ASDA and Somerfield are Turckheim only. Sainsbury's runs to an indifferent blended wine from Hugel and an own-label Gewurztraminer, while Tesco and Safeway offer own-branded Alsace selections too, indicating precisely how seriously they all take this region. Waitrose manages better, buying from the fine co-operative at Beblenheim, while Majestic have chosen a less well-known producer called Bott-Geyl, but essentially nobody is getting out and finding the individual growers who contribute so much to the region's reputation.

And yet there is more variety and versatility in Alsace than in the Languedoc, where large combines and Australian winemakers pour out a slick of identical wines year on year, or indeed than in Australia itself, to which Oddbins devotes such extravagant quantities of shelf-space, with row upon row of Chardonnay jostling tier upon tier of Shiraz in protean over-fecundity. Not only does Alsace produce a range of varietally labelled wines offering an array of genuinely heterogeneous flavours, but the wines are hardly ever oaked, making a refreshing change from the unvarying pabulum of oaky Chardonnay. Additionally, in Crémant d'Alsace, the region makes what is certainly the best traditional-method sparkling wine in France outside Champagne itself. And yet still the buyers can't be tempted to venture any further afield than a yearly season ticket to Turckheim. It isn't even as if Alsace is that far away.

Probably the greatest failure of all, though, is in California. To many, myself wholeheartedly included, the west coast of America – not just California, but the more northerly states of Oregon and Washington too – now constitutes the most dynamic and variegated wine scene outside France, and certainly the most exciting of the non-European countries. Here, there are Pinot Noirs to rival much of what Burgundy produces in its precariously uncertain climate; Cabernet Sauvignons of richness and complexity, once fraught with indigestible tannin but now full of elegant balance; oaked Chardonnays that manage to combine lushness with a savoury rather than sweet edge, as well as exhilarating generosity of fruit; Merlots plump and ripe and free of the stalky hardness of so many European offerings; snappy dry Rieslings with true varietal character; head-turningly beautiful Viogniers to square up to the best of the northern Rhône; together with a proliferating host of Italian vari-etals that are better than the humdrum norm in Piedmont and Tuscany; and of course the California state speciality of Zinfandel, which can be a touch sweet and jammy from some producers, but in the right hands acquires an opulent, velvety depth of ripe fruit and spice. The phylloxera epidemic that struck much of California's vineyard land in the 1990s meant widespread uprooting of diseased vines – a calamity that, in France, would have had vinegrowers blockading the autoroutes until the government bailed them out. In California, however, the obligation to replant was seized on by many growers as an opportunity to plant a greater diversity of grape varieties, and as the new vines start to approach maturity the range of wines on offer has begun to broaden.

Of this giddying versatility, we see next to nothing on the British high street. We get the wines of E. & J. Gallo of course, biggest single wine-producing company on the face of the earth, whose top-of-the-range offerings can be commendably complex enough. Their everyday quaffing wines, however, are insipid specimens. Gallo's Turning Leaf wines, which so many of our retailers have taken to their hearts, are sickly with unfermented sugars, and come nowhere near Orlando's Jacob's Creek wines from Australia that are pitched at the same undemanding market. Robert Mondavi, a fine producer in Oakville, California, produces a bottom-end range called Woodbridge, again sweet and simple wines of no charm or personality, but gold-dust to the British buyers. Blossom Hill and Garnet Point are even worse than Turning Leaf: bottom-end wines without a shred of class. Even the famous old Paul Masson jug wines can still be bought quite widely. All these are examples of wines doing their level best not to startle anybody with unusual flavours or noticeable intensity, and that UK retail buyers have flocked to them is an indication that their sense of adventure is missing when it comes to America. Why do their companies even pay for them to go to California if all they're going to come back with is Gallo? (The only universally listed California wines of halfway decent quality are those of Fetzer Vineyards, although even some of their varietals – such as Eagle Peak Merlot and Echo Ridge Sauvignon Blanc – are decidedly ordinary.)

The usual objection when one criticises the threadbare state of our big retailers' American listings is that the quality American producers have priced themselves out of the market, and that Chardonnays at £10 won't sell. But almost everybody lists Rosemount's Show Reserve Chardonnay from Australia at a penny short of £10, and there are white burgundies at around that price too. In any case, not all wineries do charge the earth for their wines, and if journalists on a press trip can encounter wines that would sell for less than £10, then how come these seem to escape the attention of the retail buyers? Another part of the problem is that many of the so-called boutique wineries in California and the Pacific Northwest are producing wine from relatively tiny plots of vineyard and, so the retailers argue, there wouldn't be enough to spread throughout their UK outlets. They can't, however, have it both ways. If they will take Chilean Cabernets that sell for £15 and distribute them in 30 branches, why can they not do the same with premium California wines? But they don't. The Columbia winery in Washington State, founded in 1962 and now owning great tracts of land, makes a versatile range of fine varietal wines (although, as so often in America, its Sauvignon Blanc is a neutrally flavoured disappointment). It has the production volumes to reassure the supermarkets, as well as competitive prices, and would at a stroke enliven their American ranges if they stocked a few of its wines. But they don't. It's Turning Leaf and Garnet Point all the way. Leave these ditchwater-dull wines on the shelves, and perhaps the retailers will get the message. The British wine trade has long boasted that its catholicity is what enables it to sit at the top table in the wine world, but when it comes to the wines of the USA, you are without doubt being excluded.

For whatever reason, the wine buyers have decided that there are whole categories and types of wine that we don't want. In many cases, to be sure, these are wines they have tried and largely failed to sell. This is the defence they invariably mount when one queries the paucity of decent sherry or the absence of single-estate German Riesling. Certainly, it would be wrong generally to expect them to offer the top wines of Bordeaux and Burgundy, but then again, there is a willingness on the part of some of the multiples to try their luck with Chilean and Australian wines up to a price-point of about £15, at which level a fair quantity of pedigree French wine could be had. The First Quench chain that comprises Thresher, Victoria Wine, Wine Rack and Bottoms Up is, at the time of writing (September 2000), listing a Chilean Cabernet Sauvignon – Errazuriz Don Maximiano – at £17.99 at all its outlets, but the correspondingly priced clarets and burgundies are mostly restricted to Wine Rack or Bottoms Up. Price is understandably a determining factor in deciding what to sell at which branches. Tesco lists some thoroughbred claret, as well as the odd fine burgundy and premium bottlings from some of the southern hemisphere producers, but restricts their availability to barely more than three dozen stores out of a group total of over 650. Clearly, there is no point in them giving over shelf space to £25 wines in areas where there is no market for expensive wine. These wines are always proudly displayed at the press tastings, however. In their autumn tasting of 1999, Sainsbury's showed an enormous line-up of champagnes in readiness, they said, for the millennium celebrations, but many of them were only available at fewer than 100 of the group's branches, and some of the most opulent of all at a mere 20 stores. Nothing irritates the readers of newspaper and magazine wine columns more than arriving at their local branch of a supermarket or off-licence and being told that the wine recommended in the Sunday paper is not stocked there. When I received a letter from a reader who had experienced precisely this problem at one of the big supermarket chains, I contacted their press office. If the reader cared to go into his local branch again, I was told, it could be ordered from the nearest branch that stocked it. This he did, and was now peremptorily told that if the individual branch manager had set his or her face against the delectably scented, and not overpriced, Condrieu I had recommended, then it would never be allowed through the door. Sorry. I was left to suggest that my correspondent bought his wine elsewhere.

Clearly, then, the retailers do not deserve to be judged on what they sell at a handful of their most favourably located branches, but on the core range that everybody gets, and it is here that the overall picture becomes a lot more monochrome and dull. It is as though the buyers have fixed notions about the kinds of wines the public wants. We shall look in greater detail at some of these factors in later chapters, but above all I can only see an overwhelming presumption in favour of certain Australian international winemaking consultants who can turn out reliably similar wines, whether they are made in Portugal, Argentina, Italy or even Uruguay. A dash of oak flavour –

whether from maturation in actual barrels, or from one of the oak derivatives discussed in Chapter 5 – is thought an advantage for nearly all wines, as is high alcohol. The number of wines, especially reds, labelled at 13.5% has noticeably increased over the last decade, as though customers won't feel they are getting their money's worth unless a wine has a high intoxication factor. This is not to disparage the wish to become intoxicated (what else was wine about in the first place?), but it does ignore the fact that certain wines don't need high alcohol to be outstanding. To this trend we may partly attribute the decline of interest in German wines, some of the finest of which, from the Mosel particularly, are hovering at scarcely more than 7% ABV. Alcohol can contribute weight to a wine (although not necessarily body, which is a different matter), but it rarely adds complexity. And sweetness, officially a despised taste to those who have grown out of Liebfraumilch and light Lambrusco, is very much still in evidence, in the super-ripe Chardonnays from certain Australian, South African and Chilean vineyards and in the pitiful selections from California the high-street buyers confine themselves to.

Curiously, while the white wines ideally have the oaky sweetness that is presumed to be today's preferred taste, the red wines are frequently – even where oak-softened – dust-dry with immature tannin. This is because the high-street buyers have largely abandoned the idea of acquiring parcels of mature wine, and are working to far more savage financial imperatives than would allow for maturing at least some of it themselves. If even a fraction of the vast stock-holdings of the supermarkets were to be given over to certain lots of premium reds, so that the customer could confidently open a bottle and find it ready to drink on the day of purchase, an immense service would be done to the appreciation of wine in this country. Instead, the conveyor-belt from the winery door to the supermarket shelf moves at a dizzying pace, and so the onus is on anyone who wants to drink these wines at their peak to start a wine cellar. That in itself would be a heartening development, but will never happen, and so a vast quantity of red wine – as well as a smaller proportion of white – is drunk every year in a state where it has hardly begun to develop. This is, if not a tragedy, at least a crying shame, but it is a trend that the supermarkets in particular have fostered by selling younger and younger wine. Virtually no Bordeaux or northern Rhône reds worthy of the name are drinkable within their first three years of life, and yet, trawling through the lists of the main retailers in the summer of 2000, I found next to nothing widely available from these regions made before 1998. With the wines of the so-called New World, the problem becomes excruciating. These wines are axiomatically assumed to be quicker-maturing than their Old World counterparts, but it ain't necessarily so, and why should it be? They are, after all, made in hotter, more dependable climates than those of western Europe, and have con-comitantly higher levels of dry extract and tannin. In many cases, they will need even longer to come round than a medium-bodied claret or a burly Hermitage – and yet they are sold even younger. When a wine labelled Reserve Cabernet Sauvignon or Reserve Merlot is on the high-street shelves about nine or ten months after it finished fermenting, as is notably the case with certain Chilean bottles, one has to ask what 'reserve' is actually intended to signify. Rioja Reserva must at least be aged for a minimum statutory period in barrel and bottle before it sees the commercial light of day. The South American wine industry has rendered such distinctions mean- ingless, and their Reservas seem to be straining at the leash to be on the market in time for their first birthdays.

To some extent, we must blame the wine producers themselves for this. If they weren't prepared to sell wines frequently so immature that they are still prickly with residual carbon dioxide from the fermentation, then the retailers wouldn't be able to pile up their shelves with them. But here again, the commercial dialectic is more complex than at first sight. In many cases, the temptation to sell under- age wine is so great precisely because it slashes the production margins of the winery. Sold wine is wine that isn't tied up in stock any more, and if buyers with multi-million-pound budgets to back them up are offering to lock you into a contract that will run for year after year, the rapid turnover and guaranteed income are too good to pass up. The retailers habitually deny that they do guarantee repeat purchases to wineries in certain parts of the world, and insist that if a vintage comes in sub-standard, they will exercise their right to buy elsewhere. But even without a guarantee there does seem to be remarkable continuity from one year to the next in the identities of the producers on their shelves. The Turckheim co-operative in Alsace, Gallo wines of California, Bouchard père et fils in Burgundy, Cecchi in Chianti, not to mention the huge Australian conglomerate, Southcorp, all appear on the shelves year after year in both good and not-so-good vintages. Marks & Spencer collaborate with a négociant company called Paul Sapin, which happily makes wines in Burgundy, Beaujolais, Languedoc, the Rhône, Bordeaux, the Loire and south-west France for them, branching out enterprisingly into Germany and even Australia as the buying department requires, while the Girelli combine in Italy turns its corporate hand to the diverse regions of Puglia, the Veneto, Abruzzi, Tuscany and Piedmont. As at September 2000, all M&S's South African wines were made by either the KWV or Vinfruco, all their California offerings by either the Bear Creek winery or R. H. Philips, and every single New Zealand wine by Montana. Whilst these relationships may not be regulated by guarantees or long-term contracts and do not have benefits for the consumer, they can be habit-forming. One of the drawbacks of this is that the wines available to the consumer seem to be dictated by who the producer is, not how good their wines are that year.

Sometimes ubiquity can be an index of consistent quality. Louis Jadot in Burgundy (especially its white wines), the La Chablisienne co-operative in Chablis, Paul Jaboulet in the Rhône, Georges Duboeuf in Beaujolais, Rosemount in Australia and Santa Carolina in Chile are all good producers with a record of many more hits than misses, but where a company is making a range of wines in different regions and even countries, one can't expect the quality to withstand comparison with the best wines of those based in one appellation or region, and making nothing but its permitted wines. (This picture is somewhat different in the non-European countries, where even quite small producers have traditionally bought in grapes from regions at considerable distances from where they are based, and still made admirable wine from them.)

Regionality in wine is itself somewhat of a vexed issue these days. While some have called for the entire system of controlled appellations to be scrapped as a bogus bit of originally Gallic protectionism, others (including me) have counter-claimed that the only way forward for non-European wines is to adopt some sort of system analogous to the French AOCs. Only when a particular region or district name has been protected by law do we stand half a chance of knowing what minimum quality we can expect from its wines. What we are increasingly being offered by the multiple retailers, however, is wines that don't appear to come from anywhere in particular, other than one or another country. We have already castigated Blossom Hill and Garnet Point, but there are many, many more. A glance through price lists at the end of 2000 turns up Ash Ridge and Fox Wood (from France), Chapel Hill (Hungary), Devil's Rock (Germany), River Route (Romania), Oak Village (South Africa) and Copper Crossing (Bulgaria) – names that, by their very Anglicisation, announce that these apparent place-names are really nowhere in particular. There is something irredeemably gauche in a Languedoc wine calling itself Ash Ridge, rather as the British used to call Livorno 'Leghorn', and one cries shame on the producers for submitting to the tendency. What this is really about is not creating a sense of regional identity, but rather bringing back branded wine. We may once have known the only Hungarian red wine we thought we would ever taste as Bull's Blood, but look what happened to it. It got brushed aside as soon as we started learning about wine in a grown-up way. To these ersatz place-names, the Dunroamin and Mon Repos of the wine business, are now added a host of more obviously non-geographical brands, the latest soused with some idiot marketing manager's infantile idea of humour. Wouldn't it be a wheeze to call a French wine Wild Pig? Here it is, a vin de pays d'Oc made from Shiraz (Shiraz, please note, not Syrah, the grape's

French name) alongside Fat Bastard Chardonnay, Utter Bastard Syrah, and even a Grenache-Syrah blend called Old Git — all available in the high-street multiples. No doubt this is all being done in the age-old interest of taking the pomposity out of wine ('I thought with the salmon tartare, we could begin with a vigorous young Fat Bastard, and then go on to that rather mature Stinking Frog with the braised rump') but it ends up just feeling like somebody's dork sense of humour being rammed down your throat.

As well as laugh-a-minute brand names, there are now peculiar packaging and marketing concepts to be reckoned with, too. Blue bottles, once thought fit only for Blue Nun Liebfraumilch, have made something of a comeback, and may be seen wrapped around various products from Kaituna Blue New Zealand Semillon-Sauvignon to Harvey's Bristol Cream Sherry (well, it was always going to take something desperate to make *that* commercially interesting again). An Australian Chardonnay called Pendulum comes in an opaque silver bottle to disguise its paralysing dullness. And why stick to the same old recipes? M&S achieved a first in 1997 when they commissioned one of their contract winemakers in the south of France to produce a vin de pays de l'Hérault rosé blended from Chardonnay and Merlot, the maceration on the skins of the Merlot grapes producing the right come-hither tint of lipstick, and with an appreciable degree of residual sugar. Sweetish pink Chardonnay at £3.99 must have seemed like a marketing department's dream, but it bombed. Humouring every last absurdity of the UK retail trade brings the French producers no credit: they must now be labouring under the haunting, inescapable feeling of having had their noses well and truly rubbed in it.

This sort of marketing in any case deserves a shrewder, more intelligent approach. An American winemaker, Randall Grahm of Bonny Doon Vineyards in Santa Cruz, California, made a reputation for himself some years ago by offering wines with names that made punning reference to certain French wines. There was a Grahm Crew white, a Mourvèdre red called Old Telegram made in homage to the Rhône's Domaine du Vieux Télégraphe, and a red wine, Le Cigare Volant, named after the UFOs that the winemakers of Châteauneuf-du-Pape have forbidden by local decree from landing in their appellation. There were also ice wines of a kind made by a process called cryoextraction and labelled 'vin de glacière'. But it is one thing to draw attention to genuinely innovative and excellent wines, and quite another to pursue novelty for its own sake, or dress up mediocre slosh in embarrassing gimmickry.

What has happened in the last few years to cause the wholesale mediocratisation of wine in the UK is an insidious two-way process. The trend towards international styles of wine has been supported by the buying power of the high-street multiples, and vice versa, with the result, in many cases, that even wineries that don't hire Australian consultants to make the wine have begun to produce it to a formula that suits the buyers' taste. Acidity is either cut down by artificial means or else disguised by leaving in residual sugar. Tannin in red wines is minimised where it can be, but tolerated if it means getting young wines on to the market that much quicker. Of the myriad of grape varieties the oenological profession once had at its disposal, we are slowly but surely being restricted to the same basic few, as indigenous vines are pulled up all over Europe to make way for the more commercially lucrative Chardonnay, Cabernet Sauvignon, Merlot and Sauvignon Blanc. Even where indigenous varieties live on, they are often gingered up with a dose of something more internationally recognisable in the blend. Thus do all the Macabeo-Chardonnays and Tempranillo-Cabernets come to light. Sometimes this trend has resulted in measurable improvements in an underdeveloped wine region, but the risk it always carried, the chicken now coming home to roost, is the loss of diversity in the high street. At one supermarket press tasting in September 2000, we were shown wines made by one much-travelled Australian wine consultant in South Africa, Tuscany and Puglia, while a peripatetic compatriot had contributed wines from Portugal, Spain, Argentina, Sicily, Puglia and Uruguay. Some of these wines, one had to concede, were quite good. Others were stultifyingly dull. The point, though, is about too much power being concentrated in too few hands, and the complicity of the retail buyers in underpinning that tendency. It is indeed possible for international consultants to make wines in the northern and southern hemispheres at opposite ends of the year, but when one man is credited with having made wines in Portugal *and* Sicily, or Argentina *and* Uruguay, in the same vintage, our scepticism is inevitably aroused. A certain amount of winemaking by telephone is undoubtedly going on, and the effect is much the same as when a garlanded chef with his own establishment starts opening branches with his name on them the length and breadth of the country. The thinner an individual's talents are spread, the more his or her idiosyncrasies become a familiar formula, and the less a striving for excellence distinguishes what they do. As monotony begins to set in, there is the Safebury's wine-buyer at the door, cheque-book in hand and ready to spread this monotony all over the UK high street. If the brave new world of wine was won in the 1980s in the high summer of an unsustainable economic bonanza, this is how it was lost – in the drear chill of creeping standardisation.

There is no need to take my word for it, though. The most reliable and objective way of judging this phenomenon is to look at the results of the International Wine Challenge. The IWC is a mammoth tasting event run in May every year by *WINE* magazine. Wine merchants of every type are invited to submit their best offerings to a complex but rigorous tasting procedure. The judges are a professional mix of wine trade personnel, journalists, sommeliers, members of the Institute of Masters of Wine and so forth. I myself participated six years running, and can vouch that the tasting conditions are as scrupulous and as fair as I have come across anywhere. It is up to the wine merchants who enter wines to choose from around two dozen categories. All wines are tasted blind in small flights of bottles. Each panel of six judges tastes and evaluates the wines privately, and then proceeds to a discussion. By consensus, each wine is awarded a mark. Below a certain level, the wines are thrown out. If a wine is deemed worthy of a pat on the head, it receives what the Challenge organisers used to call a Commendation, but is now termed a Seal of Approval. If the wine is held to be better still, and worthy of an Olympic-style gold, silver or bronze medal, it goes into a second round. At the very top of the quality tree, a wine may be awarded a Trophy, indicating a supreme example of its kind. Major disagreements are rare, but when they do occur, a panel may call upon one of the roving adjudicators. At no stage, however, is the identity of the wines made known to the judges. The system works. In my very first year, I held out single-handedly in defence of a very tough, tannic Cabernet Sauvignon. To the exasperation of my fellow-jurors, I was vindicated by the adjudicator and the wine was put through to the second round. Burning curiosity now made me break the rules and take a peep at the bottle. It was a California Cabernet from the small but highly respected Renaissance winery in North Yuba. Subsequently I looked up the previous year's results, and found that this self-same wine in the same vintage had been a gold medallist twelve months before. In other words, there is enough healthy disputation at the Challenge to ensure that the more difficult wines do indeed receive their just deserts.

Even adding in the Challenge's controversial Seal of Approval category, which seeks to recognise a certain level of humdrum acceptability in the wine trade, and meant that in 1999, out of 8,500 wines tasted, a total of 5,274 wines received an award of one sort of another, this still leaves well over 3,000 wines with naught for their comfort. But if the Seal of Approval wines may be assumed to be just decent, basic, drinkable stuff with no particular faults but no particular merits either, then the number of unre-markable or unacceptable wines rises to 5,500 of the 8,500 submitted. In other words, something like 65% of the wines entered in the competition are mediocre or worse. This is not my judgement on what the UK wine trade is selling. It is a verdict pronounced year upon year by juries of more than 450 tasters, many of them involved in buying and selling the very wines that are being condemned: that an awful lot of very dull, and frankly atrocious, wine is sitting on the shelves of the British wine trade. You may very well be opening a bottle of it tonight. Don't let anybody tell you you've never had it so good. It simply isn't true.

Chapter 2

YOU PAYS YOUR MONEY . . .

Or: Do you get better wine if you spend more?

SOONER OR LATER, IF YOU'VE been paying attention in the wine shop, you will notice that there are some bottles that look more or less the same as the ones you are used to buying, and were made in the same vintages, from the same grape varieties, but appear to cost considerably more. If your idea of how much a bottle of wine should cost is as fixed as the matter of how much a CD or a T-shirt should cost, then the thought of spending more than your habitual four or five pounds may never seriously enter your head. But you will nonetheless eventually find yourself wondering what these other wines taste like. A question I have very often been asked is, quite simply: Does a wine with a £50 price tag taste ten times better than one with a £5 label? Even more crucially, *why* is this wine £50, and that one only a fiver?

I should say straight away that I am not talking here about bottle-matured antique vintages, where the wine has ceased to be a bottle of wine and become a collector's item, an investment that the buyer may well hope will secure a higher return when it is eventually sold on. In my view, a case of wine bought at auction for private cellaring and resale has been as cynically denuded of its function as a Cézanne that goes straight from the sale-room into a bank vault. (By all means, hold on to the wine until it is ready to drink, but if you aren't intending to drink it, then you are not truly a wine-lover.) Everybody can understand why a bottle that is 50 years old will be expensive, but many wines – and they do tend to be the ones that crop up in the auctions later on in their lives – are already expensive on release. Are they worth it, and if so, why?

Before we can begin to answer those questions, it is interesting to consider what qualities a wine might have that would persuade a novice or inexperienced wine taster that it was indeed better. The experts talk of complexity, potential longevity and length as being the hallmarks of fine wine, and these are perfectly valid points. By complexity, we refer to the overall range of flavours that a wine possesses. A simple wine is one where there may be a dominant fruit flavour the palate quickly tires of, or alternatively, one where there is no particular flavour of anything (think of standard inexpensive Italian dry whites) but an indefinable feeling of freshness that just about suffices to make it appealing. A complex wine will offer scents and flavours in dazzling array – perhaps a wisp of wood smoke first and then a piercing fruit impression such as squashy-ripe raspberries, and then something vaguely spicy like pepper or ginger. If, in addition, the wine has a sturdy structure with plenty of acidity (and, in the case of red wines, tannin) backing up that repertoire of aromas and flavours, then it is possible to say that the wine should have a long life ahead of it. As it develops in the bottle, moreover, those initial flavours will intensify and change character, lending the wine even greater complexity. Wine tasters always look for length in a serious wine as well – that is, the degree to which the flavour lingers on after the wine has been swallowed or spat. A wine that may seem promising on the nose and palate may often betray its rather humdrum pedigree by finishing short, leaving very little for the taster to contemplate once it leaves the mouth.

This is all well and good, and represents the sort of expertise that anybody seriously interested in the subject should aim at. Finding these qualities – complexity, longevity and length – in a wine that has indeed cost only £5 is one of the great joys of today's wine market. But what, you may wonder, is the first quality to strike somebody who admits to knowing nothing at all of these technicalities as indicating a wine that is clearly a cut above? What would be the first clue? The answer, I believe, is very little to do with flavours and finish. It is, primarily, a *textural* characteristic. To the untutored palate, the first thing that impresses about a smarter wine is that it seems softer and gentler on the palate than a cheaper wine. This was very much my own earliest experience of more opulent wine. In the days when it was possible still to buy French country wines at £1.49 a bottle, I went halves with a friend on a bottle of red from a supermarket discount bin that had been knocked down to £5. 'Knocked down', please note: this was wine for which customers had originally been asked to pay in the region of six or seven pounds. It was called Fleurie, which, we found out from Hugh Johnson, was something to do with Beaujolais, and although I can no longer remember what vintage it was or who made it (I imagine Georges Duboeuf will have had a hand), I do remember we couldn't believe how soft and silky it was to drink. It had, of course, nothing in the way of tannin, since even the top *cru* Beaujolais tends not to, but as it was being reduced to clear, it must have been sufficiently mature to have lost the crunching acidity that characterises youthful wines made from the Gamay grape.

This palate-friendly gentleness of texture was all too seldom found in everyday wines in those days. In a mysteriously non-technical bit of jargon, the newspaper wine columns would sometimes recommend wines as 'a good quaffing wine', or 'eminently gluggable', which was the wine writer's code for 'beneath me at any rate, but you may well enjoy it'. And such wines very rarely lived up to these billings. Once having tasted a wine – a red in particular – that didn't assault the taste-buds with hard tannin or jagged acidity, it was hard to go back to the rough-and-supposedly-ready stuff. The same phenomenon eventually befalls wine drinkers on a learning curve when it comes to champagne. Almost everybody starts out by saying, 'Champagne's wasted on me, actually. I can't see what all the fuss is about. Tastes like battery acid – and at that price you can keep it'. This is a true and fair verdict on bulk-produced 'cheap' champagne, exactly the sort most people will have encountered at a mass-catered event like a wedding where the hosts have understandably tried to economise. The first time champagne really convinces anybody as to why it has accrued its reputation and price is when a bottle of unexpectedly mature non-vintage is bought from a retailer with a low turnover in it. Then suddenly it's all honey and yeast, and the acidity has softened to the point where it is no more than a freshening edge to an otherwise sumptuous, lushly effervescing nectar.

The dilemma facing wine consumers, however, is that it is overwhelmingly the cheaper wines that are intended to be drunk straight away, and the more expensive wines that are expected to be cellared for several years. Splashing out, therefore, on a wine costing four or five times what you would normally pay for serving at a momentous dinner party may well be a bad investment, in the sense that it will taste overly dry, austere and hard as nails – convincing enough as a serious wine, in other words, but just not much fun to drink. There are exceptions to this disobliging rule, mainly high-end dry white wines such as burgundy or reds from the southern hemisphere where there is often naturally higher ripeness and sweetness in the harvested grapes. But buying a classed-growth claret for opening at less than five years old is virtually always a mistake.

Assessing whether an expensive bottle is worth the outlay must depend on a number of technical aspects of its production, which we shall explore shortly. The primary point for the consumer, though, must simply be whether he or she likes it. If it's only cost you £2.99, and you think it's indigestible rubbish, it was too expensive. By the same token, you might be vaguely aware that a wine does indeed exude a certain amount of ineffable class, but just not particularly like it. Oz Clarke and Jilly Goolden used to make this point rather effectively during live appearances at food and wine exhibitions by inviting a handful of people to come up from the audience and taste two wines. The bottles were disguised, and labelled only A and B, but the participants were told that one of these wines retailed at £3, while the other was £50. Could they spot the difference? There was never unanimity, and there was always at least one person who picked out what might be a simple Bulgarian Cabernet Sauvignon as the expensive one, while declaring that the Château Lafite-Rothschild tasted like a £2.99 quaffer. The implied moral was that the person at whom the audience was guffawing for getting it wrong was the real winner, because to them a cheap Bulgarian red sampled without sight of the label – the very one, after all, that they could afford – tasted like £50-worth of wine.

Those who might have been tempted by the likes of *premier cru* Puligny-Montrachet, the classed-growth châteaux of the Médoc and Sauternes, Australia's Grange Hermitage, or one of the breed of new-wave Italian wines known as the super-Tuscans, may still find themselves wondering why it is that these wines sell at such inflated prices. Do the winemakers literally just charge what they think the wines taste as if they are worth? Or are there genuine economic factors at work in their creation? Do you, when all is said and done, get better wine if you spend more money? Or is it all just another kind of label snobbery, on a par with the designer clothes industry? To investigate these issues, I shall look at a handful of representative wines from the upper price brackets, including some of very recent historical provenance, and ask whether what's in the bottle lives up – pound for pound and sip for sip – to the admission fee charged.

An adventurous oenophile who had just won the rollover lottery jackpot might decide to go straight in at the deep end by investing in a quantity of wines from the Domaine de la Romanée-Conti (DRC) estate in Burgundy's Côte d'Or. There is plenty to choose from, among the reds at least. The estate makes six reds, all of *grand cru* status (Burgundy's highest quality designation): Echézeaux, Grands Echézeaux, Richebourg, Romanée-St-Vivant, La Tâche and Romanée-Conti. The last two are *monopoles*, or wholly owned appellations. In other words, the DRC is the sole producer of those wines. There is only one white wine, also a *grand cru*, Le Montrachet. When these wines are released, they are offered at prices that reflect the tiny quantities produced, and are sold on strict allocation to buyers who mostly have proven track records as DRC customers. Some of these people may never actually drink the wine, but merely realise a profit on it a few years later, while a fair proportion goes to the restaurant and hotel trade, chiefly in France.

If our lottery winner had been successful enough to bag a case via the DRC's UK importer, Corney and Barrow of London SE1, he would find there are prices to suit all pockets. The Romanée-Conti may seem a trifle steep. It is normally released at a six-bottle non-duty-paid case price of around £3,000, working out with duty and VAT at about £650 a bottle. Still, that's better value than buying a mature bottle in a restaurant. When film actor Johnny Depp bought a bottle of the 1978 to drink with a special companion in a Mayfair restaurant in January 1999, he was relieved of £11,000 for the privilege. At least Depp may have been drinking the '78 at its peak. The trio of businessman who ran up a £13,000 bill for dinner with a few bottles of wine in Le Gavroche the year before, donated the greater part of their bottle of the 1985 to the staff, on discovering it wasn't really ready to drink. The other reds are charged at considerably more modest rates, however. La Tâche can be had for the more manageable sum of around £230 a bottle, while Romanée-St-Vivant, at about £165, is something of a steal. If thrift is your middle name, the Echézeaux at about £72 a bottle is the entry-level wine. Le Montrachet, the white wine, goes for round about £500 a bottle, but its quantities are the tiniest of all, and it is almost never available to casual customers – other than in a restaurant, of course, where mark-ups may well inflate it into the region of £1,500, depending on the vintage.

That these wines are so agonisingly expensive is down to a complex of different factors. By no means the least is that they are priced to take advantage of the demand for them. When a world of wine investors is beating a path to your door, who are forced because of the very modest production quantities to compete pugnaciously against each other, you obviously sell to the highest bidder. However, this was not always the case. It was once the practice at the estate to sell the wines in mixed cases that would include one bottle of the prized Romanée-Conti alongside eleven bottles of the less illustrious *crus*. That policy, while scrupulously democratic for the general buyer (if such a person exists in the rarefied world of the DRC), seriously annoyed the Japanese investors who were beginning to exercise powerful economic influence in the fine wine market by the late 1980s and early '90s, with the result that, with the very fine 1989 vintage, the estate decided to release its wines at prices more accurately reflecting the market value. And then, quite as if Bacchus, the god of wine, were smiling down on them, 1990 delivered an even better vintage. The release prices of the Domaine's wines set a new record, one that has been broken regularly since. (In 1990, the asking price for Romanée-Conti itself was

£550 a bottle. By the release of the indisputably charming '96s it had
swollen by a further £100.)

But how did they come to command such inflated prices in the
first place? Here, history plays a part. The vineyard now known as
Romanée-Conti was first designated as producing particularly note-
worthy wine by its monastic owners in the early sixteenth century.
Later in that century, for the first of many times in its history, it was
sold off to a private buyer. By the mid-seventeenth century it had
acquired the name La Romanée, in acknowledgement of an important Roman archaeological find in the district, but the suffix came
about when in 1760 it was sold into the nobility in the person of the
Prince de Conti. The aristocratic connection inevitably meant that,
thirty years later, it was confiscated and auctioned off by the Jacobin
regime following the French Revolution. Following its acquisition by
the Duvault-Blochet family in 1869, more vineyards were added to
the estate, making up eventually the portfolio of wines available
today. It is currently owned jointly by two families, the de Villaines
and (since 1942) the Leroys, but in 1993 one of the co-directors,
Lalou Bize-Leroy, left and established her own vineyard holdings
nearby. There she now makes the only wine thought seriously capable of rivalling those of DRC for quality (and retail value). There
being no such thing as bad publicity, the value of the DRC wines
went on steadily rising through this period of turmoil. And so to the
immense commercial covetability of the wines can be added the
cachet of a glamorous historical pedigree.

That, of course, could not have come about had the Romanée-
Conti vineyard land itself not been thought worthy of purchase by a
succession of well-to-do buyers over the centuries. Its limestone and

clay soil, and its southerly aspect in the northern Côte de Nuits section of Burgundy's Côte d'Or, are geologically by no means unique, and yet historically the vineyard does appear to have been responsible for producing wines of uncommon richness and power. Burgundy is a cool northerly climate, and the sole grape variety of its red wines, Pinot Noir, ripens only with difficulty in many vintages. A vineyard that in this unpropitious environment seemed reliably to produce wines with full-blooded healthy colour and sumptuous textural depth would naturally come to be highly valued. Undoubtedly, however, the Domaine capitalises on these advantages, with a number of high-cost viticultural and vinification techniques.

In order to ensure maximum ripeness in the grapes, harvesting is carried out as late as possible. When the picking does begin, it is done by hand rather than by mechanical harvesters – a slower, but more accurate, means of bringing in grapes at optimum maturity. The yields obtained from the vines are extremely low, as little as 20 hectolitres of juice per hectare of vineyard. (Standard yields elsewhere are two-and-a-half to three times this.) Not only is the harvesting a loftily unhurried matter, but the vinification itself is too. The wines undergo a slow fermentation designed to maximise the uptake of fruit flavours and tannin from the grapes. Then comes the oak-ageing. DRC buys and seasons its own oak for a period of three years before it is fashioned into barrels – in contrast to the usual practice of buying ready-made new barrels, or even barrels that have been used for one or two vintages by another producer. Each vintage is given entirely new barrels for the oak maturation. Even the temptation to age the tiniest proportion of the wine in a previous year's oak is resisted; all the barrels are sold on after one year's use. The average length of time the wines are oak-aged is eighteen months. Such a long period, coupled with the exclusive use of new oak, are exceptionally rare in Burgundy, but it is thought – and accurately so – that the wines have the sturdiness to support and benefit from such robust, lavish treatment.

But the overarching consideration is that these wines are built to last. Potential longevity is possibly the most powerful determinant of a wine's value. If it is being sold with the guarantee of a long period of evolution, during which it will change in the bottle beyond recognition, improving all the time, then it will not only continue to put on monetary value as it matures, but also turn into something great and memorable for those intending to drink it at its peak. It is generally felt that the DRC reds can comfortably take fifteen years in their stride – indeed, positively demand it to show at their best. The simple fact of durability makes any wine more valuable than one cheerfully meant for drinking young. What you are buying is a product that is very much alive, inchoate perhaps, but all the more tantalising.

Does all this add up to £650? In pure financial terms, no. Romanée-Conti could quite easily be sold for a lot less. But the market – which is to say its plutocratic upper echelon – will pay that price, and more, no doubt, so that is how much it costs. In this sense, it has almost stopped being wine, and become simply another commodity in the luxury goods sector. That is a pity, because the wine is actually rather good, just not £650-good. But in the final accounting, whether it is an expensive wine depends on how long it takes you to earn that money. If it's three weeks' wages, you don't need it, not because you wouldn't necessarily appreciate it, but because it simply isn't worth that much labour. If it's small change, go ahead and try, but only – please – because you love burgundy and want to see what one of its finest practitioners is capable of, not just because you can. That is undiscriminating vulgarity.

Hopping over to the opposite side of France, you might decide, especially if you have a sweet tooth, to pick up one of the luxurious *cru classé* dessert wines of Sauternes. Displaying their lustrous amber-gold hues proudly through bottles of plain glass, these are wines that are hard to resist, for all that the syrupy, super-ripe intensity of a fine vintage may mean a little goes a very long way. Hard to resist, that is, until you see the price-tag. There may be some comparative bargains among the top wines (i.e. wines that cost only £20-30 a bottle on release), but at the top of the tree, and in a classification all of its own under French wine law, sits Château d'Yquem, a wine that rejoices in the designation *premier grand cru classé*. Yquem starts its retail life at somewhere in the region of £120 a bottle. Why?

In the case of sweet wines made by the method used to produce Sauternes, there is a more readily appreciable reason. Sauternes is made from grapes that have over-ripened on the vine, to the point where they are chock-full of natural sugars. As the late summer begins to fade, the autumnal mists that linger over the vineyards in the early morning leave a sprinkling of damp on the grapes. Eventually, that makes them start to rot with a type of fungus known as botrytis. As the grapes rot on the vines, they shrivel up, losing their natural moisture content but not their prodigious levels of sugar. When they are finally picked, what goes into the hods are leathery-looking little slivers of pure oozy sweetness, each yielding at the press only a dribble of concentrated viscous must that will slowly ferment up to the higher reaches of the unfortified alcohol range.

Since not all the berries on a bunch of grapes will rot at the same rate or to the same extent as each other, at harvest-time the grower is faced with a decision. Do you wait until there is a reasonably advanced set of botrytis, and then go through the vineyard taking the merely sweet grapes off along with the rot-affected ones, or do you (in conformity with good *cru classé* practice) make two or three separate pickings, allowing the less advanced grapes to hang for another few days? At Château d'Yquem, in a good year, they may make as many as ten or a dozen separate *tries*, or passages through the vineyard, effectively harvesting grape by grape. There are two immediately obvious financial implications. First, it is clearly costlier to pay vineyard workers for twelve picking sessions than for two or three, and secondly, since every berry is given the chance to develop full-blown botrytis, the yield of juice – and therefore wine – from each vine is ruthlessly minimised, down to a pitifully small nine hectolitres per hectare. The famous formula is that, in a particularly good year, one vine will produce no more than a single glass of wine. That means not only that Yquem is a fairly scarce wine (especially since it isn't produced at all in the lesser vintages), but also the vineyard must earn its costly keep through sky-high prices.

When the vinification is finished, the wine is matured in brand-new oak casks, exactly as Romanée-Conti is, but for a period of no less than three-and-a-half years. And then, far more than a dry wine, it has immense ageing potential. In fact, botrytised wines like

Sauternes are probably the longest-lived unfortified wines of all, because the high natural sugar in the wine, allied, in the case of Sauternes, to a dash of Sauvignon Blanc in the blend to give a balancing edge of acidity, means that the top vintages can go on developing for a century and more. Single bottles of nineteenth-century wines occasionally come up for auction and sell for thousands of pounds, but specialist outlets like Fortnum and Mason's or Selfridge's wine departments offer odd bottles from the 1950s or '60s for about £600. That makes £120 for a bottle of the new vintage a snip. The complex of flavours in fine Sauternes can be astonishing, even in youth. As it ages and deepens in colour to the shade of burnished antique mahogany, it becomes a sensationally beautiful wine. Unhesitatingly, I would say that good Sauternes is worth the ridiculous prices asked for it. Its labour-intensiveness shines as intricately as the workings of an antique clock. Cheap sweet wine, by contrast, is a waste of money. Buy a bag of barley sugar instead.

No expensive wine has achieved more widespread acceptability than champagne. There may be bargain fizzes in the supermarkets (which we shall look at in greater detail in a later chapter), but everybody knows that champagne is what you drink when you come into an unexpected sum of money, or when an occasion is thought sufficiently auspicious. You could spend your £25 on a bottle of classed-growth claret, but champagne's added advantage is its bubbliness, the attribute that identifies it so closely with celebration.

There are many factors that make champagne expensive. It is made by a fairly complicated process it has exported around the world, and that has become the benchmark for any sparkling wine with pretensions to grandeur. This involves producing a secondary fermentation in the bottle. Whereas other sparklers may have their carbon dioxide trapped in the wine by a second fermentation in sealed tanks, or by chilling the wine to arrest the first fermentation and then bottling it under pressure (as with Italian Asti), for champagne, the bottle the wine was first transferred into is where it all takes place. This results in two by-products, one desirable and one not. The first is the carbon dioxide that gives the wine its fizz; the second a glutinous deposit of dead yeast cells that precipitates out into the wine. Allowing that deposit to sit in the wine confers an unmistakable yeasty richness – a process known as autolysis. Non-vintage wines are given at least fifteen months on their yeasts, while three years is the legal minimum for a vintage-dated champagne. Nonetheless, when the period of lees-ageing is judged to be complete, the deposit must be removed. By a process known as *remuage*, the deposit is gradually coaxed into the neck of the bottle by a progressive tilting it until it accretes on the underside of the crown cap – the only closure the wine has at this stage. When it has collected just where the cellar-master wants it, the neck of the bottle is flash-frozen so that the yeast deposit is suspended in a little column of ice at the top. In a spectacular piece of dexterity, the crown cap is then struck off the bottle, carrying the ice and the sediment with it. After topping up, the cork is put in.

These were once lengthy manual procedures. Cellar-workers with uncommonly strong wrist muscles used to have to twiddle hundreds of bottles manually every day, directing the yeast deposits painstakingly down into the necks. The striking-out of the frozen deposit was a gruelling, messy and occasionally hazardous process that also took a long time. But ever since champagne first became fashionable in the seventeenth century the industry has been resourceful at cutting corners in what is an absurdly elaborate wine-making method. Though some champagne houses still use manual *remuage*, manual *dégorgement* to remove the yeasts is now very rare. But most commercial houses have now mechanised the production process. *Remuage* is carried out in machines called *gyropalettes*, in which bottles are turned *en masse* in large metal crates controlled by computer, while the *dégorgement* is done via a kind of assembly-line. Even the traditional method of producing pink champagne, by a meticulously judged maceration of red grape skins in the white juice, has now been all but eclipsed by the simple expedient – preferred by the overwhelming majority of rosé producers – of adding a slug of red wine to the bottle. Indeed, this is the only context in the whole of French wine law in which ready-made wine may be added to another wine in the making.

Nobody pretends that the equipment needed for making mechanised champagne is cheap, which is why the industry is now researching ways of inducing the secondary fermentation without leaving a problem deposit in the wine, thus removing the need for the *remuage*. But it is clearly cheaper than teams of cellar-workers carrying out the various procedures by hand.

Furthermore, while vintage champagne is traditionally only made in the better years, which in the cool, unreliable climate of northern Europe may be few and far between, the non-vintage market is there to sustain the leaner times. And whereas a producer of still table wine facing four successive mediocre to dreadful vintages, as the *champenois* did from 1991 to 1994, might be reduced to tearing his hair out, because a red or white wine without a year on the label is widely and rightly held to be inferior to a vintage bottle, vintage champagne accounts for only a tiny fraction of the market. We accept that most of the fizz we buy from this region will be non-vintage blended wine made to a theoretically consistent style. NV champagne is the industry's massively beneficial insurance policy against poor vintages.

In short, there is actually no decisive reason for champagne to be as expensive as it is. Technology has to some extent made it more affordable in real terms over the past century, and yet the occasions on which the price has actually come down are about rare as appearances of Halley's comet. Most scandalously of all, the industry operates differential pricing policies depending on the market it is selling to, and gullible British importers have long been charged some of the highest premiums of all. In an analysis carried out in December 1999, British wine writer Jim Budd compared Belgian retail prices for some of the top names in champagne with those prevailing in the UK. Perrier-Jouët was selling for the equiv-alent of £14.50 in Belgium, as against an average £20 in Britain, Moët & Chandon for £14.34 (£21), Laurent-Perrier for £14.18 (£22), Taittinger for £14.34 (£24) and Veuve Clicquot for £15.88 (£24.50). We shall return in a later chapter to the question of whether champagne is still a better wine than its rivals from else-where in the world, but if you have decided beyond doubt that you prefer it, you are being cheerfully fleeced every time you buy it.

Perhaps, after all, nobody is especially surprised to see French clas-sic wines selling at astronomical prices, but when an Italian wine labelled *vino da tavola*, i.e. table wine, costs upwards of £20 a bottle, then preconceptions are quite definitely being challenged. A new breed of Italian wines made in Tuscany, and christened by the British wine press the 'super-Tuscans', began to appear in the 1970s. These were Italy's explicit attempt to shake off its dowdy image as a bulk-producer of indifferent everyday jug wines, of which the alleged Tuscan classic, Chianti, was too often a prime example. The genre was established by two wines that first came to light commercially in the seventies, namely Tignanello, made by the illustrious Antinori house of Florence, and Sassicaia, brainchild of the Incisa della Rochetta wine dynasty from just outside Bolgheri, but also marketed by Antinori. What each sought to do was to create a blended red wine to equal a classed-growth Bordeaux in both magisterial intensity of flavour and potential longevity.

Sassicaia in particular marked a radical break with Tuscan tradition. It is composed principally of Cabernet Sauvignon, like the wines of the Haut-Médoc in Bordeaux, and was grown on vineyard land that had virtually slipped through the net of the rather slapdash Italian DOC structure (the rough-and-ready equivalent, formulated in the 1960s, of France's *appellation contrôlée* system). Not only did it owe its character to a French grape variety rather than one of Italy's indigenous types, but it was also barrel-matured in small *barriques* of French oak. Up to this point, the standard maturation vessel for Tuscan reds had been huge barrels of Slovenian oak, used again and again from one vintage to another, that imparted nothing in terms of oak flavour to the wines produced in them. Tignanello did acknowledge its regional pedigree a little more closely. It was made right in the middle of the Chianti Classico heartland, and was a blend of 80% Sangiovese, the local speciality and mainstay grape of Chianti itself, bulked with some of that beefier Bordeaux Cabernet. It too was matured in new French oak, lending the sharply defined red-fruit acidity of Sangiovese a creamier, vanilla-toned woodiness quite unheard-of in the wines of this region. And because they contained more Cabernet Sauvignon than the regulations allowed for, and because (in the case of Sassicaia) they were grown outside any demarcated DOC zone, simple table wines was all they could be described as on the label. What might have seemed a commercial drawback – the very humblest designation of *vino da tavola* – was turned to ironic advantage.

So successful was the marketing of each of these wines by Antinori that they spawned a host of imitators. By the 1980s, it seemed as though nobody with any serious ambition to produce quality wine in Tuscany was interested in the official DOC rules. Cabernet Sauvignon flourished in these blends, as did Merlot and even Syrah from the Rhône valley, and the French cooperages that supply barrels to quality producers the world over suddenly had a new and extremely lucrative market in the heart of Italy. As a quality movement, the super-Tuscan revolution has been an unqualified success. The initiative has been exported to other regions, most notably Piedmont in the north-west, where the classic red wines Barolo and Barbaresco were generally of much higher quality than the mass of commercial Chianti, but hardly in tune with international tastes. Sassicaia was rewarded for its trail-blazing efforts in the mid-1990s by being given its own DOC as a sub-region within the overall new DOC of Bolgheri. Grape varieties permitted for DOC Bolgheri wines include Cabernet Sauvignon and Merlot, unthinkable only a generation before, while the wine itself has proved fully worthy of the status dreamed up for it by its founders. A vertical tasting the Circle of Wine Writers organised in the early 1990s of every vintage of Sassicaia to date showed that the wine is indeed as long-lived, as complex and as fascinating in its development as great claret, against which its price seems not in the least rapacious. Along with Tignanello it was a necessary innovation, and merely tasting either of them side-by-side with even supposedly superior Chianti Classico is to be transported across a quality chasm of dizzying breadth.

Not all the fall-out from the super-Tuscan phenomenon was necessarily healthy, though. The commercial trajectory these wines described, becoming classics within a very short time-span, so that older vintages were soon as sought-after at auction as some of the great names of Bordeaux, exerted a powerful influence on producers outside Italy. If a combination of French grape varieties and French oak, big tannin and plenty of fruit flavour, could produce towering, memorable wines amid the backwash of weedy, watery, wicker-flask Chianti, then might not other regions be capable of the same upgrading on the backs of totemic premium-priced wines made in what was now fast becoming identified as the international style? The last decade has seen a rash of such wines from areas that didn't actually need to follow this example, and that are in danger of casting a pall of cynicism over the perception of quality wines.

Chile is a case in point. There are probably more top-value wines being produced in Chile today than anywhere else outside Europe, and its modern wine industry has come to maturity by carving out a series of recognisable regional styles all its own. Chilean Merlot is one of the most reliable varietal red wines in the world (for all that some vineyards have now discovered that the grape they thought was Merlot is not the textbook Bordeaux variety at all, but another, much less familiar specimen called Carmenère). Furthermore, there are wines available in the £4-5 price bracket that offer the same drinking pleasure as wines costing easily twice that and more from regions like California and South Australia's Coonawarra. But suddenly, there has been a rash of premium wines, some of them the products of joint-venture agreements with growers from elsewhere. The Mondavi winery of California has teamed up with Caliterra wines of Chile to make Seña, a Cabernet-based blend selling for an arm and a leg. Miguel Torres, the Chilean arm of the Torres wine estate of Catalonia, has recently introduced Cordillera, a premium blend selling for over £12 on release on its UK launch in early 2000, notable for containing a majority proportion (60%) of the Carignan grape variety. Carignan isn't much revered these days in its southern French heartlands, but Torres is making a virtue, indeed a USP, out of the fact that this is the first Chilean wine to be sold abroad constituted mainly from Carignan. There are others, priced even more optimistically.

It is not that these wines are of unacceptable quality, although some of them don't quite seem to have the necessary stuffing to age as venerably as the makers apparently intend. It is more that there is no particular need for them to be priced so expensively. We seem to have reached a point where every producer of quality wines feels the obligation to reach beyond the normal price parameters with one flagship wine intended to lead them into the fine wine sector.

Traditionally, a producer's best cuvées were labelled Reserve or Reserva, denoting that they had been aged in oak, or at least aged for longer than the lesser wines. Occasionally, a Reserve wine was one made from selected parcels of older vines or from an especially well-sited plot of vineyard, whether oak-matured or not. These designations have been understood by consumers for a long time. The appearance of wines with fanciful brand-names, and selling for inflated prices, seems an attempt to lend a spurious instant glory to an industry that had no need of it.

Back in Catalonia, the Torres estate, which had always had a pair of expensive but impressive premium wines in Mas La Plana Cabernet Sauvignon and Milmanda Chardonnay (selling at around the £20 mark), has now added to its portfolio a red wine called Grans Muralles. Made from a blend of traditional Spanish varieties led by Garnacha and Monastrell, it opened in the UK retail market at £45. A first tasting of the 1996 vintage in February 2000 revealed a wine of absolutely shocking tannic attack. For me, at least, its tannins were so immovably solid and aggressive at three-and-a-half years old as to make it quite undrinkable. Fourteen percent of alcohol didn't do anything to make it any gentler. Several hours in a decanter couldn't tame its fire, and to roll a single sip around the mouth was a painful, pointless experience. When would such a wine ever be drinkable? Extraordinarily for a producer of Torres's breeding, it seemed to be predicated on the outdated theory that as long as a red wine is stacked with tannin in its youth, it will age with distinction. The Californians left that thinking behind with the 1970s. But where, in any case, was the fruit needed to make it worth the wait? Grans Muralles, on the evidence of this vintage, is not worth anything like its asking price. It is merely contributing to the worldwide vogue for premium wines.

That there is such a vogue was made almost comically apparent in the spring of 1998, when Sainsbury's, at one of its biannual press tastings, showed a 'premium' from the Domaine Boyar winery in Bulgaria. Aged for three years in oak, it was a thin and currenty Cabernet Sauvignon from the 1990 vintage selling for just short of £7, an unheard-of price for a Bulgarian varietal, even one with three years' barrel maturation. If even bargain-basement Bulgaria, struggling to maintain market share in the post-communist era, can succumb to the baleful influence of international wine faddism, then the lunatics really have taken over the asylum.

The super-Tuscan movement ushered in a genuine quality revolution, and the wines it made possible duly garnered sufficient praise to establish themselves as contemporary classic styles. If the Chilean, Bulgarian and other premiums feel they can go the same way, good luck to them. For the consumer confronted with a southern-hemisphere Cabernet at £20, there are for the time being much wiser ways of spending the money. The truth is that four bottles of good Reserve Merlot will deliver far more satisfaction.

Chapter 3

WHAT'S IN A NAME?

Or: Does a famous label guarantee quality?

IF, AS WE SAW IN the last chapter, spending more money on a bottle of wine doesn't necessarily ensure a corresponding increase in quality, are we on safer ground if we stick to the familiar names? Since, in any case, we don't always want to spend £15, perhaps it is better to trust wines from regions that have established a reputation for themselves, with names recognisable even to people without in-depth wine knowledge.

The wines we shall look at in this chapter all fall into this category: Bordeaux, port, Chianti, Muscadet and Rioja. It could be argued straight away that consumers are increasingly turning towards varietally labelled wines from almost anywhere outside Europe, with grape names consequently the touchstones for identifying a wine's style, rather than the name of some little village (or sprawling province, for that matter) in the European hinterland. To some extent, this is true, and confirmed by some European producers outside the controlled appellations systems adopting varietal labelling themselves on the 'If you can't beat em' principle. But it would be wrong to exaggerate this trend. Even now, the majority of wine bought in the UK is made in western Europe. Australian wine may be hugely popular, but in the overall league table it is still down in fourth place, partly because the Australian wine industry can't supply nearly enough to meet the demand. And besides, there is a growing recognition in the non-European wine countries that varietalism pure and simple isn't enough. In the end, so they believe, people do want wine that bears, in the current parlance, 'a taste of somewhere', rather than just a taste of bulk-produced Chardonnay. So it makes sense to go back to the renowned appellations – regions that still shift substantial units on the export markets – to see how they measure up.

The wines we are looking at here are all well known for different reasons. Bordeaux has a great historical reputation. It has had a link to the British wine market ever since 1152, when Henry II married Eleanor of Aquitaine, and the English crown inherited the wine lands of Bordeaux as part of her dowry. During the 300 years of its allegiance to England, Bordeaux exported a substantial part of its annual production here, and many of the vineyards today forming the heartland of the region came into being. Even after its reversion to French sovereignty, the favour in which its wines were held endured, at least until continued hostilities with Louis XIV's regime in the late seventeenth century led to punitive import tariffs on all French products. Notwithstanding that, while the true-born

Englishman boycotted French and loyally drank the wines of
Portugal, England's oldest European ally, a British connection was
preserved. A short-lived strategic liaison between Scotland and
France that came to be known as the Auld Alliance kept Bordeaux
wine flowing to the British mainland. Not even war against the Sun
King, nor indeed the periodic Anglo-Gallic spats of the European
Union era, such as the recent *guerre du boeuf*, managed to undermine
the lasting affection that a certain kind of British wine connoisseur
has for Bordeaux, especially the region's red wines that it has
referred to for at least the last four centuries as 'claret'. If the cul-
turally iconic dinner dish of patriotic John Bull was the roast beef of
old England, then what he preferred to drink with it was claret, and
the finest money could buy.

The success of port is intimately bound up with the relations
between England and France during the ninety years of prohibitive
trade tariffs against France. English merchants scouring the Iberian
peninsula for replacements for claret developed a taste for the wines
of the Douro valley in the north of Portugal, which – although
undeniably somewhat more rugged and fiery than the best of the
Médoc – were nonetheless felt to have sufficient character for the
robust English constitution. The only problem was that they were
that much further away geographically from their intended markets, meaning that the chance of spoilage on the Atlantic sea routes
was that much greater. The answer lay in the form of brandy. If the
wines had a slug of grape spirit added to them before shipment, not
only were they rendered stable (the higher alcohol now killing off
any remaining yeasts, preventing re-fermentation), but they now
tasted even beefier than before. In some genuine sense, then, port

is an English invention, and although its production has been carefully refined since the eighteenth century, British producers have
long been an important part of the local industry. John Bull may
have switched from drinking claret with his beef to port when
France was the enemy, but, once the Napoleonic wars were done
with, port found its place as an after-dinner tipple. Gentlemen
drank it with their cigars after ladies had retired from the dinner
table, or else they retreated into clubs where women never set foot
and drank it by the bottle until the gout set in.

The other wines in my present list – Chianti, Muscadet and
Rioja – all became famous in the twentieth century when continental tourism became affordable after the war. Travellers to,
respectively, Tuscany, Brittany and the tourist traps of northern
Spain brought back a fondness for the local wine in an era when
wine was only just beginning to trickle down the social scale, and
tastes were very much exploratory. The abiding image of Chianti in
a squat little bottle encased in a wicker *fiasco*, or flask, was derived
as much from the 1960s boom that made the Italian trattoria a
familiar feature of the British high street. Its contents accompanied
everything from bowls of minestrone sprinkled liberally with dried
Parmesan to those bubbling tomatoey pasta dishes that all seemed
to have the same sauce, whether they were called lasagne, cannel-
loni or ravioli. When the bottle was empty, it served as a
candlestick. When the time came to put away sweet German wine
with other childish things, Muscadet was considered the height of
sophistication among white wine drinkers, its rapier-like acidity
and neutral bone-dryness posing the same sort of challenge to
British taste-buds as earthily pungent garlic butter or a white-hot

vindaloo curry. Rioja came even later, largely through a vigorous 1970s marketing strategy. Its soft-textured, oak-smothered unctu-ousness made it instantly appealing to people who wanted a red wine without the gritty tannins of young claret or the hard acid edge of *fiasco* Chianti.

What has each of these famous names been getting up to since?

BORDEAUX

In February 1999, a world-shaking (or at least wine trade-shaking) event took place in London. A large gathering of wine writers, including nearly all the newspaper wine correspondents, turned out for a tasting organised by a highly respected Bordeaux wine company in a private room at the Bluebird restaurant on the King's Road. The theme of the tasting was Bordeaux Brands – in other words, the bottom-end sector of the Bordeaux market. Far removed from the rarefied heights of the *crus classés*, these are wines that sell under a brand name rather than traditionally under that of a château. They are intended as entry-level products for the general consumer, wines that might offer a glimpse of the majesty of the region's aris-tocratic offerings, even as a form of introduction to the basic range of flavours to be found in a wine from Bordeaux. That said, their names reflect their market positioning: many seem to be making an effort not to appear French at all, let alone to come from Bordeaux. Amongst others, we tasted wines called Rivers Meet and Merchant's Bay, Salmon Run and Four Corners. There were twelve dry white wines and seventeen reds. The wine company had included their own Sirius brand in both red and white versions, but the remainder were from other companies. The vintages were mostly 1996 and

1997, but there was a pair of '95 reds and one odd non-vintage blend. The tasting was blind, that is to say, the bottles were disguised so that nobody knew what was what. Following the tasting, the journalists sat down to lunch for the company's UK export manager to find out our conclusions.

The result was a vinous bloodbath. With one or two cautious exceptions, the wines were swept aside. The whites were roundly condemned for lacking freshness or complexity, the reds for unpalatable dryness and bitterness, and both for a pitiful paucity of fruit. The average asking price for these bedraggled specimens was £5-6, with the bill topped by Mouton-Cadet red and white at £6.99 each. We are talking here about wines that were not merely a little dull, although a fair few did just scrape into that bracket, but rather, actively repellent. Among my notes on the white wines are such descriptions as 'smells of soluble aspirin, sulphur, ghastly cardboardy unfresh palate, abysmal' (Four Corners Sauvignon 1997) and 'cheap-smelling, washed-out pointless wine, no more interesting than industrial Soave' (Mouton-Cadet 1997), while the reds included 'ghastly stink of old wood and mustily unripe fruit, flat dispiriting palate, hard and stalky finish' (Yvecourt 1996) and 'dank fishpond nose, sickening stale seaweed quality, very off-putting, hard, tannic, fruitless' (Maître d'Estournel 1995). At the time, those four wines were selling, respectively, at Tesco, Victoria Wine (although Mouton-Cadet is widely available), Tesco again, and Oddbins, but there were many others almost as bad. The Tesco offerings were both retailing at £4.49, the Oddbins one at £5.99, and the Mouton-Cadet at £6.99. These notices would be appalling enough for sub-£4 wines from the former Soviet bloc, but for houses that are making *premier cru* Château Mouton-Rothschild and *deuxième cru* Château Cos d'Estournel for their more plutocratic customers, they are an indictment. With Chilean and Australian Cabernet Sauvignon, Chilean Merlot and New Zealand Sauvignon Blanc available in this price bracket, who would honestly choose to buy these shockers, other than people who continue implicitly to trust the name of Bordeaux, and perhaps imagine this is what wine is supposed to taste like? And yet, sales of Bordeaux at precisely this level – branded wines – rose by over 50% in 1998. Would it be too much of a conspiracy theory to attribute some of that increment, at least in English-speaking countries, to a wine called Merchant's Bay or Salmon Run sounding as though it comes from exactly those parts of the world against which Bordeaux now feels it has to compete?

Later in the same year, the consumer magazine *Which?* held a comparative tasting of Bordeaux wines selling at under £10 a bottle. Out of three dozen wines tasted, precisely three found their way into the just-about-acceptable category, and the remainder were condemned as poor to atrocious. The response of the Bordeaux industry was to suggest that British wine buyers were to blame for purchasing such dross, quite as if it were somebody else that was producing it.

Despite the plummeting reputation of branded Bordeaux wines, they continue to sell. Around 200 million bottles of wine in the branded category are produced each year, and nearly half of it is exported. Of those exported bottles, around 10% comes to the UK. We are the second largest importer of Bordeaux wines in volume terms after Germany, and the biggest of all specifically for white Bordeaux. That the UK is a market that matters to Bordeaux can be seen in the allocation of funds the region's controlling body, the Conseil Interprofessionel du Vin de Bordeaux (CIVB), made for advertising its wines here in 1999 – 14 million francs (£1.4 million). What this largely bought was an extraordinary press and billboard campaign in which the kind of soft-focus sexual imagery more associated of late with ice-cream advertising, together with free-floating fragments of text about 'lip-staining kisses', attempted to create the impression that Bordeaux wine was the last word in sensuality. Even *if* it tasted like soluble aspirin.

To understand why branded and less expensive Bordeaux is so bad is simply to acknowledge the power of a bullish market. A great many winemakers in the region are simply not making drinkable wine. Furthermore, in a region already producing far more wine than any other part of viticultural France, yet more land is being planted with vines, on the spurious grounds that some of it was once planted back in the nineteenth century, and therefore has every right to be so again. Vineyards are being allowed to bear too heavily for the lesser wines, which is why those wines at the tasting were so dilute and feeble and lacking in fruit. When the wines receive their *appellation contrôlée* status each year, the badge is awarded to a producer's entire crop: the wines are not tasted tank by tank. This inevitably means that inferior batches go out on to the market with the same quality designation as the better ones. To compound the problem, as long as the message that these wines are not worth drinking only leaks out occasionally through exercises like the *Which?* tasting, then the everyday consumer won't know any different. (By and large the newspapers won't let their correspondents take up editorial space telling the readers what *not* to buy.) It all adds up to the most vicious of circles.

As a postscript to the rancorous events of 1999, the CIVB asked its London PR agency to organise a debate in December that year, in which a panel of industry representatives offered themselves to the mercy of the press. In the course of the meeting, they announced a number of modest but significant policy initiatives designed to weed out the unsatisfactory wines. Among them was a plan described in English as 'Downstream Control', under the terms of which CIVB hit-squads will gather samples of Bordeaux wine from all over the world – from the growers, the merchants, the wholesale distributors, supermarket shelves and restaurants – and take them back to the region for blind tasting. Wines that are considered to come into the lowest of four categories of quality will become the subject of an investigation with the responsible producer. The hope is that, in future years, a producer may offer his wines for certification tank by tank to avoid a repetition of the ignominy. (Or perhaps he'll just go back to wine school.) It is not expected that this system will bear fruit for about five years, and it is by no means watertight. With the Bordeaux industry officials judging their own wines, there will inevitably be a tendency to leniency, and of course, as was pointed out during the debate, bad wines will only be tracked down once they are already on sale to unsuspecting drinkers, but the scheme is indubitably progress of a sort. Despite the initial buck-passing, the terrible press that Bordeaux received in 1999 in the UK did penetrate. It all started at that February tasting. I can think of few comparable occasions at which I have better justified my existence as a paid wine commentator.

PORT

Despite the best efforts of the PR industry, port is saddled with a number of unfortunate associations. Apart from being the tipple of gouty old duffers in gentlemen's clubs and elaborately hatted ladies who offset its syrupy hotness by mixing it with lemonade, it has always been inextricably linked with thunderous hangovers. At first, as its 20% alcohol steals around the belly, it seems to have a comforting warmth, and the Benylin-like stickiness of its sugar content helps the medicine go down. Drink too much, however, and you pay the price the morning after, because it is thick with congeners, the substances in red wines and the darker spirits like whisky and brandy that contribute to the state of toxicity known as a hangover. These include traces of methanol, or wood alcohol, derived from the cell walls of the grapes, and higher alcohols generated by yeasts from amino acids in the fruit. Congeners are significantly more potent than ethanol, or ethyl alcohol, itself, even though they are present in comparatively tiny concentrations. The problem is that they also contribute a great deal to the aromatic presence and overall character of a wine or spirit, which is why vodka, which contains very few of these substances, has little character compared to cognac. Therefore, the better a port is, the more likely it is to contribute to a congeneric hangover.

It isn't as though port is a particularly nice idea for a drink. There is no getting around the fact: it is a half-fermented red wine with a slug of industrial grape spirit in it. Raising the overall level of alcohol kills off the sugar-consuming yeasts while they are in the middle of turning the grape-juice into alcohol, which means that a quantity of half-finished grape sugar remains in the wine. Compared

to the winemaking process accorded to fine table wines, port production is fascinatingly slapdash. It is virtually the only type of wine
left in the world that is routinely made by treading the grapes.
Vineyard workers clamber into the stone vats and gradually subside
up to the tops of their legs, squelching laboriously away in the gunge
for up to three hours. This is sweaty work, the more so because, as
the mass of squashed grapes starts fermenting, heat begins to rise off
it. After about 36 hours, when the sugar level in the juice has
declined to around half its original concentration, it is pumped out
into another vat primed with the grape spirit. Once strictly a
Portuguese product itself, this spirit may now, as a result of an EU
ruling, be bought anywhere on the open market, the only stipulation
being that it has to be a minimum of 77% alcoholic potency. None
of this process makes it sound like an especially sumptuous wine.

At the top of the tree sits vintage port, which accounts for no
more than 2% of the region's production, and is only produced in
years when the quality of the harvest is thought to merit it. Vintage
port is matured for a couple of years in wood, but then bottled and
released on to the market, and it is the buyer who is expected to lay
it down in the cellar until ready for drinking. Depending on the
characteristics of the vintage, this may easily require half a lifetime,
which is why port was traditionally given as a christening present to
a baby boy, the idea being that when he attained his majority (21 in
those days) the wine would be just about ready for broaching. (As
the new millennium dawned, Taylor's 1977 vintage port, considered
one of the very finest of the vintage, was still not ready for drinking.)

Below vintage level, a plethora of different categories has been
introduced in order to expand the customer base. Among these,

late-bottled vintage (the wines of a single year, but aged for up to six years in cask by the shipper and intended to be ready on release) and aged tawny (essentially the same thing but aged beyond six years until the ruby colour of youth starts dropping out) are worth drinking. The rest is largely garbage, basic bulk ruby or tawny made from grapes of indifferent quality. Basic tawny is probably the worst-value port of all. It comes mainly from inferior vineyards where the grapes take on less colour during the ripening, and thus lose it more quickly during the brief ageing. The maturation is often precipitated by leaving them in the hottest upper part of the Douro, as opposed to the cooler traditional location of Vila Nova de Gaia downriver, until they taste of heat exhaustion. What would normally be seen as a liability in other wines (other than madeira, where heat stress during production actually improves the quality, to make a much more appealing drink than port) is made into a virtue by producers supplying undiscerning markets. This coarse, caramelised taste is particularly popular in France, where such wines have for generations, unfathomably enough, been drunk as refreshing apéritifs.

Most misleading of all is a category of port called 'vintage character', a designation that deserves to be ranked alongside 'leatherette' or 'coal-effect' in the pantheon of reflected glory. Vintage character port is not the product of a single vintage, nor does it have the character of actual vintage port. It is theoretically a better-than-average ruby, aged in bulk for a couple of years longer than usual, but the regulations are so imprecise that the term covers a multitude of watery sins. It should be shunned at all costs, in the hope that the authorities will do what they should have done years ago and abolish this category. But many producers are still taking advantage of consumer confusion, especially in the UK, to encourage a belief that this thin, often raspingly rough product is only a heartbeat below the splendour that is vintage port. And if you believe that . . .

CHIANTI

A quality revolution much lauded in the wine press has swept through the Italian wine industry. It has been focused in particular on Tuscany, with the kinds of wines we looked at in the last chapter – the so-called super-Tuscans – in the vanguard. In the best two zones of the no fewer than seven allowed to call themselves Chianti, namely Chianti Classico and Chianti Rufina, some of this renewed commitment can be discerned, but for the remainder – which includes virtually everything labelled simply Chianti – the picture is unremittingly grim. Chianti is one of the least likeable of all Europe's historic wines, a pallid travesty of what it could and should be.

In 1716, in what was effectively one of the earliest examples of a wine appellation, the best zones for Chianti production were identified in an edict promulgated by the Medici grand duke Cosimo III. Not only was the Classico heartland of the region defined, an area to the north-east was also classified as Pomino (today's Chianti Rufina). These were held to be the districts where the best wines, those of great complexity and longevity, were customarily produced. Had the Chianti name been restricted to these two areas, the subsequent gradual decline in quality that in the twentieth century became a vertiginous plunge, might have turned out less critical. Even now, there is a sound argument for delimiting Chianti exclusively to the

Classico and Rufina districts, and finding some other name for the wine of the other five zones – Colli Aretini, Colli Pisane, Colli Senesi, Colli Fiorentini and Montalbano. Indeed, scarcely any of the wine made under these sub-regional denominations tastes as though it deserves the standard DOC designation, let alone the top accolade, DOCG (*denominazione di origine controllata e garantita*) that all Chianti has enjoyed since the mid-1980s. A truly quality-conscious industry would declassify all this other slosh to the level of basic IGT (*indicazione geografica tipica*), the equivalent of the French *vin de pays*, or country wine.

The other zones were generously included in the Chianti denomination in 1932, when a government commission decided that Chianti should not be seen as the exclusive preserve of a small clientele, but deserved to be accessible to a wider market both at home and abroad, and recommended expanding its geographical reach beyond its traditional area running from Florence south as far as Siena, to encompass hillside vineyards in peripheral districts around Montalbano, Pisa and Arezzo. In this respect, it was defined as a generic name, indicating a *type* of wine – treated somewhat similarly to cava, the traditional sparkling wine of Spain, also not delimited under national regulations to one exclusive region. No exercise in trying to spread quality by association across a broader catchment area than makes geographical or viticultural sense has ever succeeded throughout wine history, however – the French authorities have unwittingly reduced the overall standard of Chablis by setting the boundaries for it ever wider. Chianti was no exception, and as the region grew, so its quality and image were set on a downward trajectory.

To be fair, the 1932 law did provide for specifications as to winemaking methods, climatic conditions and grape varieties that should have helped matters. Probably its most important stipulation was that, once and for all, the Chianti blend should be based on the Sangiovese grape, as opposed to the inferior Canaiolo that had been the norm until the turn of the century. Canaiolo is a useful ingredient in mitigating some of the often over-keen acidity of Sangiovese, but doesn't as a vine variety possess enough intrinsic character for a wine intended for ageing.

Expanding the denomination was not the only action to undermine the quality of Chianti, though. The region has been plagued ever since by over-production. In the fifty years or so between the Dalmasso law and the award of the DOCG to Chianti in 1984, the annual production of the region virtually doubled, despite the area of land under vine shrinking by no less than 80%. Virtually no good wine made anywhere in the world is produced from high-yielding vineyards, and where quality revolutions have taken place, they have nearly always been predicated on reducing the vines' fecundity. Nonetheless, when much of the Chianti vineyard was replanted with new vines in the 1960s and '70s, hardly any attention was paid to questions such as the density of vines per hectare or the quantities of grapes they were permitted to bear.

Then there is the question of what goes into the wine. The principal two grapes grown in Chianti are Sangiovese and Canaiolo, but admixtures of two *white* varieties are also allowed. One is Trebbiano, one of the dullest white grapes in the world, and responsible for a huge proportion of the flatly flavourless Italian dry white sold in the mass market (its white wines have been memorably described by Andrew Barr as little more than 'a 12% solution of ethanol in water'), and the other is the *slightly* more scented Malvasia. There is some precedent for adding white grapes to classic red wines. Côte-Rôtie in France's northern Rhône is a thick-set Syrah red with great tannic presence in its youth that is given even greater complexity by some producers by the addition of the local white grape Viognier up to a fairly surprising, if scarcely ever used, proportion of 20%. But Chianti has nothing like the monumental texture or depth of northern Rhône Syrah. It is a lean, acidic creature, and all that admixtures of neutral white varieties can do is to dilute and emaciate it still further. Not all producers use the white grapes, but by no means all the more illustrious growers shun them.

Finally, the ageing of the wines by the producers themselves often helps to vitiate the already very modest quality. Although some have now adopted the commercially valuable technique of maturation in regularly renewed small oak *barriques*, the majority still prefer *botti*, giant egg-shaped barrels of old Slovenian oak, often subjected to less than impeccable hygiene routines between batches and imparting nothing at all in terms of wood complexity to the wines. The longer the wines were kept in these vessels, which in the case of some Riservas might have been as much as three years, the more dank and dried-out they ended up tasting.

The whole Chianti picture appeared to brighten in the 1990s, when the more conscientious producers began cutting back yields, using smaller, fresher barrels and eliminating the white grapes from their blends. The DOCG of 1984 also daringly allowed Chianti growers to use up to 10% non-indigenous red grapes in the blend, which in practice has meant Cabernet Sauvignon. Undoubtedly, some wines with healthier colour (most traditional Chianti has a rather dispiriting tawny hue even when young) and better cellar potential have since emerged, but to say that Chianti is once more deserving of the esteem in which Cosimo III held it is rashly premature. In 1999 I tasted a comprehensive range of Chiantis available on the British high street from all sub-regions, at both Riserva and non-Riserva level, and found the overall standard lamentable. Most of the wines are thin, hopelessly sour specimens bereft of any real fruit character, and many of the UK multiples buy their core Chianti from the same bulk producer whose basic offerings are abysmal. The buyers can't seriously like these wines. They are bought because, as a recognised name, Chianti will always sell, the more so perhaps since the vogue for Mediterranean cooking that broke upon British shores in the early 1990s shows no signs of abating. Leave it on the shelf. You don't need it. Look for Rosso Conero, Rosso di Montalcino, Montepulciano d'Abruzzo, even the Morellino di Scansano (a re-emerging Sangiovese-based Tuscan DOC) that the largest UK supermarket retailer is stocking at the time of writing, but reject that basic Chianti. At least when it was sold in those wicker baskets it was being honest about itself.

MUSCADET

The house wine of Brittany is the pre-eminent export success of the French wine industry. It is grown on about 13,000 hectares of land to the south and east of Nantes at the western, Atlantic end of the Loire valley. Much of it is consumed locally, but around half the annual production is sold abroad to markets that have seemingly never grown tired of its relentlessly dependable neutrality of flavour.

The one characteristic that marks Muscadet out, as against the similarly flavour-free whites of Italian fame, is that it is endowed with the sort of scything acidity not otherwise a noticeably popular attribute in white wine these days. It is as though that 12% ethanol solution had had added to it an incautious dollop of tartaric acid. The sole grape variety it is made from, Melon de Bourgogne ('the Burgundy melon', on account of its shape) was kicked out of the eponymous region centuries ago as an inferior drone. How on earth does a wine answering to that description continue to be popular?

In that lost era of innocence before Australian Chardonnay changed the world, Muscadet was what consumers from countries with no real wine tradition, such as the UK, switched to when they decided they had grown out of the confected, sugared-up flavour of cheap German wines. If Liebfraumilch was the instant coffee of the wine world, Muscadet was the thick black espresso. The more toe-scrunchingly acidic it was, the more you were able to prove that your taste in wine had grown up. It went to the head a little more quickly on account of its higher alcohol, but that mouth-scorching acid edge was what really sorted the men from the boys, at least the ones who hadn't gone all the way yet and graduated to red wine.

Muscadet as a region is sub-divided into four districts, by far the most productive of which is, improbably enough, about the best: Muscadet de Sèvre-et-Maine. The picture, though, is dominated by contract growers who sell their production to the négociants, who in turn actually make the wine. The growers are constantly clamouring for higher prices for their grapes, while the *négociants* have the tricky job of reminding them that Muscadet is not seen as a quality wine, and that forcing the retailers to charge more for it without concomitant improvements in standards would be commercial suicide. On the other hand, the controlling body of the region is not always noted for its enlightenment. On a visit to the region in the autumn of 1995, I was told, by one of its senior representatives, among other things:

(a) *that basic AC Muscadet is not in any sense inferior to Muscadet de Sèvre-et-Maine* – a view radically at odds with the best of the region's *négociants*, Jean-Ernest Sauvion, who says that Sèvre-et-Maine should be seen as equivalent to a *cru* wine, much as Fleurie may be compared to basic Beaujolais;

(b) *that the officially authorised yield of around 45 hectolitres per hectare could be inflated by up to half as much again, and an acceptable wine would still result*;

(c) *that the notion of lower yields producing better wine is merely 'an idea of journalists'*; and

(d) *that appellation contrôlée wines such as Muscadet will always suffer because they are not generally allowed to produce as much wine as vins de pays.*

Views such as these go some way to explaining why Muscadet hasn't a hope of being taken seriously as a quality wine.

Some authorities, whistling in the dark on Muscadet's behalf, insist that the region is changing and beginning to produce some exciting wine, pointing to practices such as barrel-ageing to support this incredible claim. Barrel-ageing a neutral, thin white wine is the last refuge of the moneyed scoundrel, as may be seen in parts of Germany and Italy. Some producers, notably the organic grower Guy Bossard, have managed to get the oak balance right by using white burgundy casks in their third year so that the wood effect is not over-pronounced, but a Muscadet aged in new oak is as horrible as seeing a tiny infant in make-up.

There is only one sure-fire way of making Muscadet interesting, and that is to age it. Buy a wine with the words *sur lie* on the label (indicating that it has not been strained off its yeast lees during the winter after vinification, resulting in a marginally softer mouth-feel), and keep it for at least five or six years. Its acidity having had the chance to soften, it then takes on the buttered green-vegetable character of a mature light-bodied white burgundy. This advice may be in defiance of virtually every wine guide ever published, but it works. An eleven-year-old wine I tasted in the region was full of savoury, hazelnutty complexity. And why stop there? In 1985, M. Bossard told me, he drank with great pleasure a 1949 Muscadet with a ripe Reblochon cheese.

RIOJA

Without further ado, I should acknowledge that there is far more decent Rioja (particularly red) around than Chianti or Muscadet. Soft-textured, strawberry-scented, and with the unctuously oily mouth-feel of ageing in American oak, it was a fine introduction in the 1970s to many consumers warily trying red wine for the first time. Since then, it has lost its way a little, though, for a number of reasons. Its commercial success in the 70s led to a considerable increase in the area under vine, and the new-fangled vineyard technique of training the vines along wires, the better to control exposure of the grapes, resulted in rocketing yields. As a wine producer Spain has always been hampered by absurdly small yields for such a benign climate, arising in no small measure because of the traditional system of growing the vines as free-standing, squat little bushes – a system now ironically being celebrated for producing more concentrated red wines in parts of Australia, as the wheel of viticultural fashion comes full circle. In the last twenty years or so, though, the pendulum in Rioja has swung too far the other way, a trend exacerbated by the introduction of permitted irrigation towards the end of the 1990s, after a prolonged campaign by many of the contract growers. Irrigation too has the effect of driving up yields. *Négociants* and co-operatives still dominate the scene, and although some turn out wines of unimpeachable quality, the generality is thin, uninspiring stuff.

Over-ageing in oak has bedevilled Rioja for generations. The wines traditionally considered its finest, the Gran Reserva bottlings, which in the case of the reds must spend at least 24 months in cask, are often tawnied, oxidised, desiccated specimens, their feeble frames supporting a ton-weight of old dry wood flavour. With the white wines it was hard to see, even in an era that suddenly went mad for the butterscotch flavours of new oak, what the point of such treatment was. Most were hopelessly oxidised by this method, the fruit reduced to a kind of dried citrus-peel pot-pourri. Marquès de Murrieta and López de Heredia are the two principal producers still making white Rioja in this style. One might emit a stifled cheer for its defiant survival, but these wines' lead-weight impact on the palate is such that more than one glass seems as insuperable as that third Shredded Wheat.

Among the more up-to-date versions of white Rioja now being favoured by the UK wine market, it is as well to look for one with a reasonable percentage of the Malvasia grape. The senior partner in the blend, Viura (known elsewhere in Spain as Macabeo), is not over-endowed with personality. Given temperature-controlled fermentation, it can turn out a nice, light, lemony quaffer, but does the world really need yet another of those? Hungarian Chardonnay may supply exactly the same, for considerably lower outlay.

More enterprising growers, making their own wine instead of selling grapes to the co-operatives, restricting yields and using wood more judiciously, are what Rioja needs. Other regions of northern Spain are making wines in the same basic range of styles from the same grape varieties as Rioja (among them, Navarra and Ribera del Duero are pre-eminent), which are undoubtedly now achieving much higher quality across the board. When Spain's new top-drawer wine designation, DOCa (*denominación de origen calificada*), was formulated in 1991, as a category analogous to Italy's DOCG, Rioja was its first recipient. The classification primarily reflects the historic importance of the region, and is granted on the principle that the prices the growers get for their grapes are substantially higher than the average paid throughout the country. In other words, if the growers can command top dollar for their production, Rioja must by definition be a better wine. This is known as putting the cart before the horse.

The five wines I have singled out are by no means the only under-performing classic wines in Europe. An extended investigation might also have sharp things to say about Chablis, about *cru* Beaujolais, about sweet Hungarian Tokaji. It is often said that it took the southern-hemisphere invasion of the European, and specifically the British, wine market to shake up these redoubts of conservatism, and galvanise them into producing wines more in tune with what consumers wanted. To a great extent, this was true. But the backlash wasn't long in coming, and as producers in the Languedoc fell over themselves to supply the wine trade with varietal wines of indeterminate regional identity, often from appallingly high yields, so the criticism of me-too-ism began to stick. That enabled those in the traditional appellations to sleep a little more soundly in their beds once more. If regional specificity was now increasingly the trend in the so-called New World – where the whole varietal movement had started – why should wine-drinkers suddenly want to go back to wines bearing no more exact geographical designation than Vin de Pays d'Oc? This, in theory at least, should be the salvation of the classic appellations.

There is much to commend this line of thinking, and I would not dissent from it, but it is all the more reason for the growers in regions that have enjoyed the imprimatur of the classic appellations to brush up their acts, and once more produce wines worthy of their names. The utter frustration felt by certain conscientious growers in Muscadet that their appellation is forever stuck with the reputation of unambitious mediocrity should frighten the life out of producers in other regions. Even Bordeaux may not be exempt, if it continues to churn out dreadful branded wines for the mid-priced sector of the market. Once a wine has become a by-word for unpalatable rubbish, it may be beyond redemption. There are still one or two fine producers in Lambrusco, for example, but who would dare to sell their wines now? And who would buy them?

Chapter 4

ANY COLOUR YOU LIKE, AS LONG AS IT'S PALE YELLOW

Or: How the world turned into a global winery

THERE IS A JUICILY ENJOYABLE story from the 1990s that tells of how a winemaking concern in the south of France called in a team of Australian consultant oenologists to overhaul its vinification methods. At the time, this was already an established practice in many of the old European wine countries. Technicians from the southern hemisphere had already ensconced themselves in parts of Italy, Portugal and Spain, and had taken winemaking procedures by the scruff of their grubby necks, advising on such practices as temperature control, pre-ferment maceration, even new methods of trellising vines in the vineyard rather than letting them sprawl all over the ground like hyperactive weeds. These interventions were beginning to pay off in that bright, palatable, fruity wines were starting to emerge from areas that had previously had no contact with such alien phenomena. Now it was France's turn.

For many – probably most – French winegrowers, the idea of letting Australians call the shots, even for one harvest only, was and is absolute anathema. This is not just a matter of a richly protean cultural history whose lineage extends back over centuries having nothing to learn from neophytes. Nor is it simply a matter of taste, although both of those factors undoubtedly play a part in the French resistance to outside influence. Rather, at bottom, there is a lingering suspicion among many winemakers that the Australian ways of doing things are simply this season's fashion, and that if they all switched over to making wines the Antipodean way, the end result would be a bland homogenisation, the reduction of wine's possibilities to a stiflingly narrow range of the same few flavours that would repeat on an endless loop from one vintage to the next.

Thus it was, we can assume, something close to soul-selling for the Domaine de la Jolie Maison faced with poor write-ups and sluggish sales, to call in the A-team, sun-bronzed Australians with a mission to clean up the lean, mean wine-streets of the Languedoc. Any number of complex technical factors might account for the undoubtedly fetid flavour of the domaine's wine. Perhaps fermentation temperatures were too high. Perhaps the wrong clonal selection had been made of the principal grape variety. Could it be that the antioxidant treatment was insufficient, and more judicious use of sulphur dioxide was required . . . ?

After a bit of preliminary nosing around, the consultants suggested that, as a prelude, the pipes used to transfer wine from the fermenters into the storage-vats should be given a quick sluicing-out. A swoosh of detergent and a good rinse later, and the new wine was pumped through. Nothing wrong with it. The Australians collected their fee, picked up their briefcases again, and headed off to their next client, leaving behind them, one imagines, a slightly pregnant silence as the chief oenologist gazed reflectively into the middle distance, and, in the way the sales director ground an expired Gitane into the dust, perhaps even a hint of reproach.

To the French, keepers of wine's holy flame, inviting in loud-voiced Australians with their talk of 'Chardie' and 'Cab Sove' and 'sweaty-saddle Shee-raz' must have been a pretty unpalatable hors d'oeuvre to the pride that was about to be swallowed. When the problem turned out merely to lie in some elementary point of hygiene – rather as if one had got a computer engineer to look at an unresponsive screen, only to watch him turn up the brightness and leave you a bill for £100 – the hors d'oeuvre must have become a rather elaborate entrée. At least there would have been a nice fresh bottle of Domaine de la Jolie Maison to wash it down with.

The phenomenon of the flying winemakers, as these globe-trotting consultants came to be known, occasioned a fairly wide-ranging debate as the 1990s progressed. They were nearly all Australians, graduates of the oenology course at Roseworthy Agricultural College near Adelaide, now a constituent department of Adelaide University. Since the vineyard cycles in the northern and southern hemispheres are a mirror-image inversion of one another, the Australians were quite capable of jetting over to Europe during the picking and fermenting season, overseeing the winemaking in a number of regions and getting back to the Barossa before their own grapes had fully ripened. Despite their initiatives meeting with the surliest welcome in France, it was among the co-operative producers of southern France that they first made their mark. The decisive turning-point is usually held to be 1987, the year in which Bordeaux-based English wine merchant Tony Laithwaite speculatively invited an Australian team to come and manage what was undoubtedly one of the more problematic French vintages of the decade. So much a part of the global winescape has the Flying Winemaker since become that Laithwaite has now registered the title, so that any oenologist clocking up the air-miles on a never-ending spin around the globe may only refer to him- or herself officially as an 'international winemaker', or some such synonym.

This trend eventually prompted the market, especially in the UK, to wake up to the ripe, sunny flavours of so-called New World wines. When I toured south-west France for *WINE* magazine in 1993, I was asked at every turn – in Madiran and Jurançon, in Tursan and Gaillac – 'What can we do to compete with New World wines?' Some producers were eager for reassurance that the fad for *les vins de l'Australie* would soon pass, and that the British would then gratefully return, their palates weary from being blasted with oak and wines with 14% alcohol, to the traditional appellations of Europe. Others, peering more clear-sightedly into the crystal ball, could see that, unless the lesser-known enclaves of southern France absorbed the lessons of globalisation and revolutionised the way they made their wines, the game was up. The French wine industry's chosen solution to haemorrhaging market share to the Australians was to make wines in emulation of them, whether this meant hiring Australians to tell them what to do, or – more palatably – doing things by the Australian book themselves. The absorption of non-European methodology to produce wines that tasted non-European was so pervasive that, as early as 1996, SOPEXA (the commercial front responsible for promoting French food and wine in foreign markets) ran a UK advertising campaign in which varietally labelled *vins de pays*, or country wines, were promoted with the slogan, 'There's a new world of French wines to choose from'. If only there hadn't already been a New World to choose from. Here and there, then, one began to taste wines that would once have sat in giant *foudres* used again and again from one vintage to another, contributing nothing other than a slight sense of oxidation, now given a short period of ageing in brand-new small oak barrels.

Imitation may be the sincerest form of flattery, but it can also be the least sincere means of flogging a dead horse. There is very little market for Coteaux du Languedoc blanc, but an unquenchably vast one for Barossa Valley Chardonnay. And so, where once it was the case that only Alsace in France made wines that were called by their grape varieties, now every other *vin de pays* south of Avignon is a Chardonnay, a Sauvignon, a Cabernet, a Merlot, a Syrah or – after the Australian fashion of double-varietal designation – a Cabernet-Merlot, a Chardonnay-Viognier or a Syrah-Grenache. That these wines are for the most part cheaper on the British high street than the equivalent Australian varietals is what has helped regional France to survive as a commercial presence. Otherwise, they could well have ended up being confined to the less lucrative export markets or to largely local consumption.

Increasingly, however, as commentators, myself included, have surveyed the changes this quality revolution has wrought over the last decade, a feeling of unease has set in. The upswing in quality that some regions of Europe – southern France, probably most of Spain and Portugal, parts of the south of Italy and the countries of the former Soviet bloc – have undoubtedly benefited from has been bought at an uncomfortably high price. That price is standardisation. This revelation first hit me decisively at a *WINE* magazine tasting in the mid-1990s, devoted, expansively enough, to Chardonnays from around the world. The tastings are always conducted blind, so that nobody may be unfairly influenced by the name on a label. The best of Burgundy, California and Australia therefore had to take their chances amongst wines in much humbler price categories from central and southern Europe and the French Midi. Inevitably, when there is no geographical clue as to the wines' origins, one finds oneself having a stab at guessing where each specimen may have come from. In the case of these Chardonnays, the exercise had become wholly, inescapably futile. The *premier cru* burgundies were not hard to spot, nor were the premium Californians, but, those aside, there was an enveloping tsunami of lightly oaked, faintly lemony, unobjectionable wines that could have been made absolutely anywhere. The only occasional clue to their origins came when a light, noticeably acidic wine seemed to be labouring under a canopy of clumsily overdone, charred oak flavour, and then one could perhaps see the influence of New World winemaking being applied to wines that hadn't got the constitution to support it. Could this besetting homogenisation be progress?

In the last few years, some writers have begun to speak out against the tendency. It isn't that we wish to go back to the old, dirty ways of regional European winemaking, or that we have suddenly discovered a passion for those traditional grape varieties Picpoul, Clairette, Ugni Blanc, Aramon and the flocks of other ugly ducklings once the staple fodder of the wines of southern France. It is more that we can't see the attraction of an unrelieved diet of the same two or three dishes, and particularly not when hopping from one wine country to another along the wine-merchant's shelves affords no relief from the same obsessively repeated flavours. The practice of calling any dry white wine Chablis, still going strong in parts of the United States (though banned, of course, for any wine sold within the European Union, other than those from the designated region of that name), or any hearty red Burgundy, or any spirit-boosted fortified wine Port, was rightly condemned by wine writers as well as the bureaucrats responsible for rooting out instances of such sharp practice. It tried to pretend to the consumer that these names were simply indicators of a basic wine style, and therefore readily transportable across national boundaries, much as the British were content to see happen with Cheddar. But what has replaced such simple-minded branding of wine is varietal labelling. Chardonnay is now the international linguistic currency of dry white wine. Of course, that means that the wine in the bottle has to be made from Chardonnay, but that's OK. Chardonnay is relatively easy to grow, withstands a wide spectrum of vinification treatments while still giving a reasonable account of itself, and everybody wants it, so you know you can sell it. What could be simpler?

Or more deadly dull?

To those who have unreservedly endorsed the internationalisation of wine, there is no problem here. The choice was between two stark alternatives: either the old, sloppily made filth of rural Europe, or the bright, technically competent, Australian-influenced style of international Chardonnay. (Unless, that is, you were the sort of unreconstructed snob who spent their money on *grand cru* and *premier cru* burgundy, and wouldn't have dreamed of buying a wine vulgar enough to have a grape variety mentioned on the label.) But this was always a grotesquely caricatured picture. It is a case pugnaciously made by BBC TV's Oz Clarke, most consistently in the Introductions to successive editions of his annually updated *Wine Guide*. Clarke is a formidably accomplished and hugely experienced taster, far more so than viewers of the hardy-perennial BBC2 series *Food and Drink* might suspect. His views are worth listening to, especially when as emphatically put as on this issue.

'The Australians are coming,' the 1993 edition of the *Wine Guide* portentously announced – coming, he meant, to those areas that had always supplied the bottom end of the market, our everyday quaffing wine:

> The thing is that most of it used to be unutterable filth, and now it's going to be fresh, bright, packed with interesting flavours – and affordable. And the chief reason is the bands of roaming Australians who increasingly consult or actually make the wines in these many corners of Europe.

Where indigenous grape varieties had no intrinsic quality, they should be bolstered by international grapes, 'Cabernet and Chardonnay, Syrah and Sauvignon'. Everything necessary should be done, argued Clarke, to flout the appellation regulations where they stood in the Australians' way, or else the authorities should tell the local winemakers the truth: that they and their successors were 'doomed'. This Introduction does also state that, 'I don't want them all to start making one international style of wine', but it isn't clear how that risk was to be sidestepped if the only answer to what he calls 'pathetic' grape varieties was to drown them, or indeed replace them wholesale, with international varieties.

By the 1995 edition of the *Guide*, this argument had shaped up into a general assault on the system of controlled appellations that is intended, at least, to guarantee quality by identifying and defining the best grapes and practices for each district:

> [T]he law is often an ass when it comes to appellations. Political pressure allows all kinds of hangers-on to famous appellations, or allows enormous generic appellations to bask in reflected glory.

This is the undeniable truth, as I argued in the last chapter, but it serves best as a criticism of the way the laws are administered, not of the system itself. It is precisely the appellation structure that has delivered the best wines in the first place – the ones that the non-European countries began by emulating after all. That is why in Australia and New Zealand, the United States, Chile and South Africa, they are all in their own ways gradually moving to a system of defined appellations in order to let the greatest wines stand out. To Clarke, this can only be a retrogressive nightmare:

> It's especially disturbing to see master blenders like Australia and New Zealand being tempted to a French-style geographically-based appellation of origin system . . . I hope these countries, and others sniffing at the appellation bait, remember that it was their exuberant freedom from bureaucratic interference that allowed them to create the flavours that the general public now loves.

The Introduction for that year closes with Clarke enthusiastically mixing up wine cocktails – a Tasmanian Chardonnay with a Portuguese co-operative white, a Napa Valley Cabernet Sauvignon with Gamay de Touraine and a slug of southern French Syrah-Grenache – and declaring all the wines improved by the exercise.

In the 1996 *Guide,* the Introduction celebrates the arrival of a piece of technology known as the spinning cone. Invented first as a quicker and more efficient method of de-alcoholising wine for the teetotal market, it has been found capable also of separating out the volatile compounds responsible for certain aromatic characters, and perhaps other essential constituents too. '[T]aken to its logical conclusion,' Clarke suggests,

> it might well be possible to simulate the flavours of wines that now claim to gain their quality from their grape variety or their birthplace. If so, the whole worldwide system of controlled denominations would become meaningless.

It is the advent of such technologies, he claims, that have made everyday wine drinkable. 'Basic wine is a beverage, a drink blended up to the specification of consumer preference.' But so, of course, is diet cola or alcoholised lemonade, and therefore the message seems to be that rock-solid standardisation is where wine ought to be heading if it is to achieve the same level of consumer acceptance as those other products.

Dismissing the appellation system as 'a protectionist marketing device aimed at raising prices and developing image', a mere bureaucrat's tool to serve the interests of the producer rather than the consumer, Clarke goes on to insist that if we say that fine wine is an expression of the soil, the climate, the place where it was grown, . . . those things don't count for anything without human commitment. Give me a winemaker who cares, and is struggling to produce good wine out of pretty unfavourable *terroir* and unsung grape varieties every time, over a lazy, cynical, lucky producer who happens to possess some revered and famous vineyard land and is prepared to milk it for all it is worth.

We can all, it is true, cast our votes against the lazy cynicism of this latter winemaker, whilst noting his uncanny resemblance to a straw target, but who is this caring, struggling figure? He or she sounds remarkably like the kind of grower for whom the arrival of those Australians, fresh off the plane and unpacking their spinning cones, has sounded the death-knell. Unsung grape varieties, we have been taught, are the sort that ought to make way for Cabernet and Chardonnay, while the effects of that unfavourable *terroir* can be rectified in a trice as soon as the cone gets into its spin cycle. Why the residual affection, then, for this benighted grower? We have just been asked to see that wine is a beverage to be tailored only to consumer demand. Surely the point can't be that the cheap-and-cheerful end of the market can make do with spinning-cone wine, while the rest of us get to savour the results of the 'human commitment' invested by the caring strugglers? What horrible qualitative apartheid would that constitute?

Back in the 1990 edition, Oz Clarke chided those high-street retailers that just listed the same wines in perpetuity because they were commercially popular. Calling for diversity, he advised the wine trade, 'We have clearly said, we do *not* want all our wine to taste the same'. The point I think he has missed in the years since then is that the flying winemaker movement and the application of certain technological procedures the world over has resulted in precisely the grim homogeneity he once set his face against. It didn't need to. It could have, and did, deliver advice on vineyard management and winery hygiene that many of the poorer areas were sorely in need of. But where it has over-ridden, or induced local producers to over-ride, the indigenous traditions of a particular appellation solely in order to supplant them with what one might call Esperanto wines, made to a doggedly invariant international formula, I shall have to be excused from the celebrations.

It is in the character of the market to reduce everything to the same basic identity in due course. The post-war Western economic system, which began by excoriating the command economies of the Soviet bloc for their denial of consumer choice, has in time delivered us a market dominated by gigantic multinational brands that exist to crush the life out of their competitors. Among alcohol products, no sector once had greater power to resist this kind of standardisation than did wine because, by its nature, every vintage delivers different conditions, and because, although the appellations have rules and parameters to be abided by, each grower expresses them in his or her own individual way. Of course, there were good and bad producers (there are good and bad flying winemakers), but at least everybody wasn't trying to do the same thing. Now that Chardonnay and Cabernet have become worldwide cash crops, they are.

If the influence of consultant oenologists were only being felt in areas starting from a relatively modest quality base, such as the

Languedoc, southern Portugal or countries like Hungary, there would be nothing startling about the phenomenon. We might indeed heave a sigh of relief that we were being offered something a tad more palatable to drink on holiday in the Algarve. But the true test of whether the world really has been turned upside-down is whether so-called New World ways of making wine have reached the most illustrious appellations of Europe. If even areas like Burgundy, Bordeaux and the Rhône are tumbling, we may be assured that the citadel is at last being stormed.

Burgundy is not often absent from the various debates periodically engulfing the wine world, and not surprisingly its red wines, made exclusively from the Pinot Noir grape variety, are at the very epicentre of this one. There is one view of red burgundy, the traditional one, which holds that the wine has no business smelling of youthful primary fruit, and that it should be closed and tightly knit until it attains a sensuous state of maturity, when it takes on an inimitable scent of decay. It is unforgettably expressed by Anthony Hanson in the first edition of his important study, *Burgundy* (1982): 'Great burgundy smells of shit'. Recently, however, that view has come to be challenged by winemakers determined to eliminate the scatological aromas of manure, old cheese or overhung game from their Pinot Noirs, precisely because they are now seen as faults and therefore undesirable.

This opposing philosophy is founded on a vinification regime emphasising early fruit characters (those heady summer scents of cherries, strawberries and raspberries that can be so appealing in young Pinot), through fermentation in temperature-controlled stainless steel, rather than the traditional open vats, and through allowing the wine a shorter period of resting on its fermentation sediments (lees). The result is a cleaner, fresher feel, making the wine approachable much earlier in its life. Earlier picking of the grapes ensures vigorous acidity in the finished wine, so that when it undergoes its malolactic fermentation, as nearly all red wines do, the transformation of hard malic acid into softer lactic won't leave the overall texture too mushy. Furthermore, it may well be given a maturation period in small new oak barrels, which have largely been shunned in Burgundy because a pronounced oaky aroma and flavour is thought to be more than the often rather fraily constituted wines can bear.

A winemaker such as the highly regarded Saintsbury in California's Carneros region underpins the pure red fruit in its Pinots by giving the grapes several days' maceration on their skins at low temperatures before any fermentation is allowed to begin. The result is wine with a gorgeous aromatic profile in its youth – musky raspberries and ripe black cherries – but which at three years old is still hard as nails with immature, crunchy acidity. In other words, while the acids seem to be trying to fool you into thinking this wine the product of a cool, northern European climate, the underlying ripeness of the fruit betrays it as anything but. That maceration period additionally encourages more colour extraction from the grape skins, and greater take-up of tannin, not an attribute classically associated with Burgundian Pinot Noir, which is generally held to be at the lighter end – in both colour and texture – of the red wine spectrum.

Those are the twin poles of the Pinot Noir debate: taut, slow-developing wines or lush, ripe creations of immediate charm. What, then, are we to make of wines like those of Joseph Roty in Gevrey-Chambertin, one of the most aristocratic appellations on the Côte de Nuits, in Burgundy's heartland? A wine like his single-vineyard Gevrey, Champs-Chenys, may be scarcely recognisable as burgundy to the lavatorial school. Its deep pigmentation, its nose of ripe raspberries and coffee beans backed up by overt oak, and – perhaps most of all – its surprisingly weighty tannins, are all far closer in style to Carneros than Côte de Nuits. Another producer from this region making wines in the same broad style is Domaine de l'Arlot in Nuits-St-Georges. Both producers' wines find favour on the robust palate of American wine commentator, Robert Parker, the man credited with starting the whole stylistic argument in Burgundy when he wrote an incendiary article in the late 1990s calling most of the region's wines a disgrace. In his characteristic tasting note, Parker praises the 'gobs of jammy, sweet fruit' in Domaine de l'Arlot's wines – exactly what many weaned on old-school burgundy can't stand. A leading British wine importer, himself now making wines in Burgundy and the Loire, stated baldly to me that the wines resulting from this burgeoning tendency are 'crap'. It may all depend, of course, on whether you prefer to smell crap or raspberries in the glass, but what vindicates this view, says the same outspoken critic, is that, 'after three years in the bottle, they fall apart'. In other words, the fruit may be on the point of breaking up while the tannins are still flexing their muscles. Here Robert Parker's summation of the Domaine de l'Arlot's *premier cru* wines, Clos de l'Arlot and Clos des Forêts, is very telling: 'Neither of these offerings,' he says, 'will be particularly long-lived'. He seems, despite himself, to be endorsing the British importer's withering view. This verdict is all the more astonishing when you remember it refers specifically to the 1990 wines, a vintage that generally produced burgundies of exemplary concentration, and therefore (at least in theory) great longevity.

At bottom, what the burgundy debate indicates is, far more than issues such as tannin extraction or the use of new oak, a relentless drive for cleanness and ripeness of fruit flavour and a consequent, almost obsessive concern with hygiene at all stages of vinification. That is the true fulcrum of this argument. Not just Pinot Noir, but also Chardonnay and Sauvignon Blanc, have been the prime targets of this puritanical approach. These are the varieties, indeed, that have been most affected by the internationalisation of winemaking. One thinks of those geographically indeterminate Chardonnays at the blind tasting I mentioned earlier. Similarly, there are producers of white wines in the Graves district of Bordeaux fermenting Sauvignon in barrel with very little, or even none, of its traditional blending partner Sémillon to adulterate the starkly pure Galia-melon quality of the fruit, and protecting the juice every step of the way from the unwanted interference of oxygen. These, too, have left customary Bordeaux practices a long way behind.

In the case of dry white Bordeaux, we might emit a smothered hurrah at that abandonment of tradition. Outside the very uppermost echelons of the *crus classés*, there were virtually no drinkable wines being produced, and poor hygiene was undoubtedly the culprit. But does all wine have to be squeaky-clean? In a world where we are coming to prize organic fruits and vegetables over their pesticide-riddled cousins, why must it be assumed that we want scrubbed and shiny wine?

Sauvignon Blanc is another case in point. In its homeland at the eastern end of the Loire valley – most notably in the twin appellations of Sancerre and Pouilly-Fumé that face each other across the river – Sauvignon is capable of producing wines that taste like no others anywhere in the world. It may not have the exuberant fruit-cocktail flavours of the mood-of-the-moment New Zealand version, but it has two distinguishing characteristics of its own. Firstly, it almost invariably has higher acidity than the Kiwi Sauvignons of Hawkes Bay or Marlborough, even though the climatic range it grows in is remarkably similar. That is because its growers are less squeamish about their wines retaining a gastronomically useful razor-edge of sharpness, and because (unlike their southern-hemisphere counterparts) it is not axiomatically assumed that they will be drunk within a year of the vintage. Still more distinctively, however, is an olfactory and gustatory note that crops up in virtually no New World Sauvignons at all, with the occasional odd exception from South Africa. It is a whiff of smokiness, an acrid wisp of something smouldering that puts the Fumé into Pouilly-Fumé, though it is quite as readily detectable in the best Sancerre. In an earlier era, when a familiarity with such things could be presumed in a boy's education, it was compared to gunflint, the striking of which on steel produced the spark that flashed in the pan during target practice. Cap-pistols and party-poppers produce the same fleeting smell: a quick, nostril-pricking plume of invisible smokiness. Oz Clarke has evocatively compared it to the aroma rising through a pavement grating from a cellar where fresh coffee beans are being roasted. Perhaps the filter-machine or espresso-maker, once it starts steaming, comes close, too. 'Empyreumatic' is the wine technicians' term, if anybody cares. It is not a barrel scent, since virtually no growers use oak in Loire Sauvignon. From whence, then, does it derive?

Some say it is a soil characteristic. There is some flint in the chalky soils of central France, where these wines are grown, and it would seem inconceivable that it doesn't impart some tasting character to the grapes. In parts of Pouilly-Fumé, in particular, there occurs a geological type called silex, in which the soil is especially rich in flint. Wines grown in these patches, considered sufficiently illustrious for the producer to be allowed to put the word 'silex' on the label, are the most monumental Sauvignons made anywhere. On the palate, their flavour range goes beyond mere fruit, and enters a sort of twilight zone of rock-hard, stony, minerally concentration overlaid with that beguiling curlicue of smoke.

It remains the case, though, that the wine can be cleansed of that acrid savour by interventionist winemaking. Cold-stabilising of the must, very low fermentation temperatures, early bottling and perhaps even flash pasteurisation can all play a part, for it remains the case that a lot of Sancerre, and even Pouilly-Fumé too, lacks any discernible trace of smokiness. It is often simply crisp, tart, aimlessly appley or lemony stuff that could have come from anywhere, and doesn't even noticeably taste of Sauvignon. Tasting a range of wines from these two appellations with a New Zealand winemaker a few years ago, I found too many of them lacked that acrid quality. Suddenly, we hit one – a Sancerre, in fact, from one of the appellation's most celebrated growers – replete with it. 'At last,' said my tasting companion: 'a wine with a bit of dirt in it.'

In California, they often call their Sauvignon varietals Fumé

Blanc, as if in homage to Pouilly's finest, but there is nothing of the flintiness of Loire Sauvignon about them. Nor is there anything, other than in a very few examples, of the herbaceous pungency of the grape. The Californians don't really like it, and thus have tried to neutralise its natural style. That 'Fumé' in the name may refer to a charred quality derived from oak fermentation, a heavy-handed treatment that, in my own view, Sauvignon doesn't lightly forgive. Otherwise, what has happened is simply that the wines have been cleaned up to remove any aromatic trace that might frighten the horses. It is a great shame that this stultifying blandness is now increasingly also seen in the wines of the upper Loire. It is yet another side-effect of internationalisation. (Incidentally, lovers of unoaked smoky Sauvignon who find themselves baulking at the bottom-line prices of Sancerre and Pouilly – around £8 these days – should set a course for the eastern European shelves. Hungary now has some impeccable Sauvignons in this style at basically half the price.)

Another stylistic idiosyncrasy in danger of being overwhelmed by the tide of international taste is a type of red made from the Rhône grape Syrah, known in much of the southern hemisphere as Shiraz. If you consult any wine guide on the characteristic taste of the major grape varieties, you will almost invariably find Syrah described as 'peppery'. It may also have purple fruits and even flowers such as violets or roses conferred on it, but all commentaries – not excluding my own – advise the novice taster to look for pepper on both the nose and palate. Sometimes we are even more specific. I see that in 1996 in my own general wine guide I warned readers to expect anything from 'a mild suggestion of spiciness at the back of the throat to the exact and inescapable smell of freshly milled black peppercorns, quite as if the winemaker had given the wine a few twists of the grinder before bottling it'. The point is that this descriptor applies almost exclusively to the wines of the northern Rhône, where the AC reds (Hermitage, Côte-Rôtie, Cornas, St-Joseph and Crozes-Hermitage) are made entirely from Syrah. In Australia, Argentina, the United States, South Africa and elsewhere, you will struggle to detect the slightest hint of it, for all that annotated restaurant wine lists still insist it's there.

If Australian Shiraz isn't peppery, we may assume that this is not an innate characteristic of the grape. Perhaps we are back once again to the question of location. Most of the vineyard land of the northern Rhône is planted on steep slopes on either bank of the river. Although this is technically southern France, the region doesn't enjoy anything like the sweltering climate of the Midi. It usually endures severe winters, and the amount of exposure to the summer sun vineyards enjoy depends entirely on their aspect. South-east-facing slopes fare the best, but not all growers are lucky enough to have them. Syrah is a thick-skinned, deeply pigmented variety that demands warm climates to ripen to its optimal potential, when it will reward the grower with massively structured, muscular wines with far greater longevity than even the burliest wines of Bordeaux to the west. In the northern sector of the Rhône, it may not achieve quite the right combination of vintage conditions more than one year in two, and yet Hermitage and Côte-Rôtie in particular are considered among the noblest expressions of this variety. Can it be that here, precisely at the margins of its feasible cultivation, it out-shines the production of Shiraz grown in far more reliable climates?

And does the marginal nature of those vineyard sites also account for the cracked black pepper in the wine?

I believe it does. What is certain is that the longer Syrah is left on the vine, the more it loses of that preternatural aromatic personality. Unless it has been a particularly beastly season, it ripens reasonably promptly anyway, so leaving it hanging in the hopes of achieving even greater intensity in the wine is both misguided and self-defeating. It is a grape that requires a natural element of acidity at harvest in order to show its paces in the winery, and give it a chance to perform during cellaring. Late picking risks a critical loss of both acidity and flavour concentration. Therefore, the most conscientious growers in the northern Rhône have tended to harvest it quite early. (The one inevitable exception is Marcel Guigal, lionised by Robert Parker as the greatest winemaker on the planet, who picks his Syrah notoriously late and yet still makes astonishing wines from it.)

In addition to picking times, though, there is the crucial question of yield. If it is encouraged to bear too heavily, as in some of its hotter locations world-wide, those piercing aromatic notes are lost. What the producer is then left with is a soupy – or even worse, stewed – style of lumpen alcoholic red that has become for some the textbook style of hot-climate, hearty Shiraz, but that bears about as much resemblance to the finesse of real Syrah as sparkling Prosecco does to champagne. In the Rhône, its yields are often very small, which is why its aromatic range is so pronounced and why it lives for so long in the bottle. One of the more affecting, even miraculous, qualities of the best Hermitage is that, even after maybe fifteen years of cellaring, it emerges with its primary fruit intact. You might, as you pour the first glass, be expecting the sweet rankness of high game, or perhaps the leathery intensity of old claret, but what you get is a uprush of perfectly ripe red and black berries, the liquorous concentration of preserved fruits perhaps, but fruits nonetheless. And pepper.

In the early 1990s, a theory about the pepperiness of Rhône Syrah did the rounds. The reason, it was tentatively suggested, that it was infused with this quality, of which most other Syrah/Shiraz was innocent, was that it was essentially not quite ripe. That would have fitted in with the tendency (*pace* M. Guigal) to pick it early on the vertiginous slopes of the Rhône. Those benighted souls who thought they were enjoying a unique and apparently inimitable style were in fact pouring unripe wine down their throats. Whether this was the sour-grape verdict of Australians, or whether it sprang from a more measured analysis of northern Rhône reds, isn't clear. What is clear is that Côte-Rôtie from a great grower, even lowly co-operative Crozes, needs no such apology or explanation. Unlike Loire Sauvignon, it has resisted the international trend and remained defiantly, confidently itself: the all-out pepperiest red wine in the world. And what else do you want to drink with steak au poivre?

There are other styles of wine, by no means exclusively French, that have hardly fought off internationalisation. One could mention Barolo and Barbaresco in the Piedmont region of northwest Italy, towering reds full of red-hot alcohol and vindaloo tannins, made from the Nebbiolo grape variety. Admittedly, nobody much wants them outside their region of origin, other than a few diehard connoisseurs of gigantically strong red wine that virtually never loses its rigid astringency, but their producers have scarcely compromised.

One exception is Angelo Gaja, now considered by acclamation perhaps the finest winemaker in Piedmont.

As long ago as the 1970s, Gaja began experimental plantings of Chardonnay and Cabernet Sauvignon, right in the heart of Barbaresco. His father's reputation in Barbaresco had been second to none, and Nebbiolo was what it had been about. Signor Gaja's now famous first reaction to the news that his son was planning to make Cabernet Sauvignon was '*Darmagi* (Such a shame!)' – so that is what Angelo Gaja called the wine. Gaja's Darmagi Cabernet became one of the talking-point wines in the 1980s. For the wines of Piedmont it seemed to point the way to an alternative future to uncommercial obscurity, and yet, having proved the point with the Cabernet, Gaja went back to focusing on what Barbaresco is expected to do. He established a portfolio of Nebbiolo reds made from single vineyard plots within the denomination. The jewels in the crown of Gaja's range are the Sorì San Lorenzo and Sorì Tildin Barbarescos, reds of unapologetic, shattering intensity containing all the chocolatey, tarry depth of flavour Nebbiolo is feted for. In Oz Clarke's view, these undoubtedly tannic, slow-developing wines are unmistakable Nebbiolo, 'but they have become comprehensible to the international palate, something that traditional Piedmont reds never were'. To me this is a far more enlightened compromise than simply giving up and starting again with Cabernet and Chardonnay. There is quite enough of that in the world already, and there will only ever be a tiny fraction that is Nebbiolo. (One might add that the triumph has been achieved by working scrupulously within the parameters of the appellation system that Clarke elsewhere professes to despise.)

Of course, wine has to develop as the world of technology, not to mention consumer taste, develops. Painfully gradually, wine-makers in some of the more hermetic European regions have realised that they can't just continue to make wine as their grand-parents did, for the baleful reason that, sooner or later, nobody — apart from the local restaurants and bars — will want it. That conceded, however, what the wine world didn't need is advancing standardisation. If unchecked, it will mean that one day, just as you can now check into a five-star hotel chain anywhere from La Paz to Pyongyang and get a Club Sandwich from room service, so you will eventually be able to ask for a glass of the local white in a wine-growing region and be given a light-bodied, mildly oaky, highly polished Chardonnay tasting comfortingly like all the others. You'll be able to have any colour you like, as long as it's pale yellow.

The winemaking consultants who have done the most constructive work are those who have worked within the regulations of their areas. There is certainly much more work to do. South-west France is full of interesting wines. So is southern Portugal. So is the south of Italy. They all deserve wider recognition, which means they all deserve to be made more competently. Do we want them all to go over to Chardonnay and Cabernet because those are the only wines the world seems to want? And if not, if we wish to preserve that diversity we all say is what we treasure about wine, then we have to realise that the appellations are our best chance of doing so. The alternative is a fate worse than alcopop.

Chapter *5*

CHIPS WITH EVERYTHING

Or: Would you like a little wine
with your oak?

I T IS A SOBERING THOUGHT that, but for reasons of pure prac-
ticality, all our wine might taste like retsina. Nowadays nobody
likes retsina, not even holiday-makers on package tours to
Greece. When, back in the 1960s, however, wine was for the
mass of society an acquired taste, it was still possible to believe that
retsina was another exotic Mediterranean speciality worth getting to
like, along with olive oil and tomato-flavoured tomatoes. Tourists
brought back the odd bottle from the Peloponnese, opening it with
friends to demonstrate just what uncharted waters they had navi-
gated in the last fortnight. Everybody would cautiously sniff at it –
'An unusual bouquet, isn't it?' – and the first tentative, bitter
mouthful would confirm what the aroma had threatened.

It was unbelievably horrible. It tasted like something to be applied to a grazed knee. If the thin pink wines of Provence lost a little something on the journey home, retsina was found even more wanting. Being offered a second glass was an undisguised dare, as challenging to one's British resilience as hundred-year-old egg or sautéed frog legs.

How on earth did any wine traditionally come to acquire such an objectionable taste? When the principal vessels available for storing wine were large earthenware amphorae, resin was what was used to preserve it. In the classical Greek and early Roman periods, therefore, this is how most wine – and certainly everything considered to be the finest – would have tasted. Pine resin was not only used to coat the insides of the jugs to make them airtight, but was also added to the wine during production to make it more muskily aromatic and, more importantly, to preserve it. Resinated wine kept longer. Ground resin, or indeed whole pieces of it, would be added to the grape juice before it had even started fermenting, imparting its pungency to the wine throughout the vinification. This is indeed how most retsina is still made today, the preference now being for steeping it whole in the pressed juice, and only removing it when the wine comes to be drawn off its fermentation sediments. With the exception of one enterprising estate in South Australia, though, this is not a style of wine imitated anywhere in the world these days outside Greece and Cyprus.

What finished resin as a taste in wine was wood. Wooden barrels are known to have been used for storing the best wines in the high-altitude regions of central Europe as early as the first century AD. It was to be some 200 years later before their use became widespread in the Roman Empire, as it was discovered that they were able to preserve wine without the need for an interior resin coat, and therefore represented a more economical proposition than earthenware jars, which were anyway weightier and less manoeuvrable to transport. At some stage – we know not when – it must have been noticed that certain types of wood, particularly new wood, imparted their own scents and flavours to the wine, and thus was the association between fine wines and barrel maturation irreversibly forged.

Exactly when oak became the preferred vehicle for wine is also lost to collective memory. Early barrels were likely to have been made of palm-wood or, in the more northerly cultures where they were in systematic use before the Romans adopted them, evergreen woods like fir. The silver fir (*Abies alba*) of the mountains of central and southern Europe, source of turpentine as well as timber, seems to have been particularly common. Not only wines would be stored in such vessels; other liquids such as oils, and precious commodities like salt, also went into them. Eventually, though, it was the malleability, watertightness and sheer strength of oak that made it the most practical wood. Although, following the demise of the Roman Empire, the technique of wine maturation was lost to European practice for many centuries, it gradually returned during the Renaissance, particularly in Germany where massive tuns of light, sweet Riesling wine were often kept in the cellars of the clerical nobility for decades, protected from spoilage by low temperatures and assiduous replenishment.

In his key work *The Story of Wine*, Hugh Johnson relates tasting a light white wine from the Stein vineyard near Würzburg in

Franconia that had been made in 1540. Since bottles with corks were not introduced until the late seventeenth century, the wine had spent perhaps its first century and a half in a large cask before being transferred into glass. The last few bottles of it sat in the cellars of King Ludwig of Bavaria throughout the nineteenth century, and were in due course acquired at auction by a London wine-merchant. One of these was opened in 1961, and the young Johnson, at the outset of his career, was able to taste it:

> Nothing has ever demonstrated to me so clearly that wine is a living organism . . . It even hinted, though it is hard to say how, of its German origins. For perhaps two mouthfuls we sipped a substance that had lived for over four centuries, before the exposure to air killed it.

A wine from the era of the European Wars of Religion and Ivan the Terrible was still momentarily alive, immaculately preserved through the centuries in wood and then glass, only finally expiring under a lethal and sudden dose of oxygen. 'It gave up the ghost,' recalled Johnson, 'and became vinegar in our glasses.'

That a wine as traditionally delicate as those produced in Germany's northerly climate could withstand such extended cask-ageing gives some idea of just how indispensable the wooden barrel had once more become to winemaking by the time of Shakespeare. Towards the end of the 1600s the introduction of sealed bottles represented a further dimension in the maturation of wine: longevity. Johnson's Steinwein was helped by its formidable concentration of sugars (1540 was a particularly hot, fine vintage – the 1961, as it were, of the sixteenth century), but brief barrel maturation followed by cellar storage under a cork stopper made the lengthy maturation of drier wines feasible.

Increasingly, though, it was not just the preservative qualities of oak barrels that were held to be of value to winemakers. During the course of the twentieth century, greater and greater attention came to be paid to the precise effects on the aroma and flavour of wine imparted by wood, according to the type of oak used, the manner of its treatment in the cooperage, the length of time the wine spent in it, and whether the barrels were brand-new or had already been used for at least one previous vintage. Wherever you looked among the classic regions of Europe, the finest wines were traditionally aged in oak. In some cases, the characteristic scent impressions a wine was expected to emit were, at least partly, to do with oak rather than any inherent quality of the grape the wine was made from. The burnt-butter aroma of fine white burgundy is oak. The creamy vanilla scent of Rioja Reserva is oak. The nutty tang of aged tawny port is oak. (In some cases, the effect is harder to separate from grape characters. Is the famous cedarwood nose of claret – sometimes described as pencil shavings, sometimes cigar-box, but always as something woody – a function of its oak-ageing? Or is it a combination of oak and the natural stalkiness of Cabernet Sauvignon and Merlot grapes grown in a cool, marginal climate? Nobody has quite decided, but certainly oak plays an integral part.) By contrast, very few of the internationally revered wine names were unoaked styles. There was Chablis, there was Beaujolais, there were the light white wines of Italy, and there was German Riesling in its various guises. When the palate tired of the enveloping richness of oaky wine – an effect perhaps a little akin to having one's fill of cholesterol-laden cuisine, when a sharply dressed, crisp leafy salad suddenly seemed a treat – at least these wines were always on hand to answer the call.

Or were they?

It was perhaps inevitable, given the insatiable demand for oaked wine that has pervaded every corner of the wine-drinking globe, that consignments of freshly charred, brand-new barrels should in recent years have started turning up at some rather unlikely addresses. Some of these experiments, such as the barrel-ageing of Soave by certain producers, have been successful, with the potential for greater versatility in the wines a genuine revelation. Others (one thinks of some of the oak-aged German Rieslings) have only smacked of desperation: strain after commercial respectability and higher returns and the result is embarrassing, misshapen creations that should have been quietly cellared by their makers and kept well away from the marketplace. 'If this is the way you want it,' these wines seemed ruefully to sigh, 'who are we to argue?' The oaky style has thus become a universal bugbear, resisted initially as anti-thetical to tradition, but then reluctantly adopted by some (enthusiastically, it must be said, by others) as the face of the future. As the use of oak has spread into unfamiliar territory, to be unoaked has suddenly come to seem rather frumpy and passé. Like the pre-middle-aged foolhardily turning, after much wise hesitation, to combat pants and facial piercings, certain growers in even such stainless-steel citadels as Muscadet have gritted their teeth and turned to oak. If you can't beat 'em . . .

Chablis is one white wine that is nearly always expected to show the clean, sharp lines of an oakless dry white, but the use of oak in Chablis is perhaps not quite as contentious as it might at first appear. It can be seen to its best effect in the wines of François Raveneau, René Dauvissat and William Fèvre, the last of whom also bottles under the labels Domaine de la Maladière and Domaine Auffray. Most consumers will associate Chablis with steely, bone-dry, relatively neutral white wines, as razor-sharp in their youth as those of Muscadet, but evolving after three years or so to take on creamy nuances, slowly accumulating complexity in the process. One of the most fascinating attributes of the best Chablis, however, particularly observable in wines from the top two quality echelons of the appellation (*grand cru* and *premier cru*) is that, with bottle-age and the concomitant loss of acidity, it more often than not appears to acquire a mouth-filling silkiness of texture hinting tantalisingly at the richness conferred by barrel-ageing. Most of it will have had no such treatment and, moreover, will have given no hint of such a development in its first flush of youth. It may seem a shame, then, when the wine is endowed with such an uncommonly individual trait, to over-egg the pudding by adding a layer of vanilla seasoning in the form of oak, but the reasoning of producers such as Raveneau, Dauvissat and Fèvre is that, precisely because the wines do have this innate ability to acquire roundness and structure with time, they are perfectly capable of withstanding – indeed being positively enhanced by – barrel-ageing and even barrel fermentation.

Maturing a wine in barrel after its transformation from grape juice into an alcoholic drink imparts a slow, relatively subtle flavour of the wood. Much depends on the type of wood used, on whether it is new or previously used, on the degree to which its interior sur-faces have been charred or 'toasted', and naturally on the length of time it stays there. A more pronounced oak flavour is contributed to a wine if the entire vinification has been carried out in barrels, including the initial fermentation. What is happening here is that a wine is being produced from oak-flavoured grape juice, rather than having that flavour applied to it later. In Chablis, both of these routes are being followed. Barrel-fermenting a wine as subtle and delicate as Chablis may seem an enterprise fraught with peril, and certainly requires great nicety of judgment, but it is by no means always misguided.

William Fèvre in particular is scarcely a revolutionary young firebrand. On the contrary, he is very much a stickler for tradition, sometime president of the Syndicat de la Défence de l'Appellation de Chablis, scourge of those who would seek to expand the Chablis appellation back into areas where no wine has been grown since the late nineteenth century, and a man whose article of faith is that what makes great Chablis is the soil – Kimmeridge, to be precise (a composition of limestone, clay and microscopic fossilised seashells, named after a village in Dorset at its northernmost geological extension). Nearly all of the 50 hectares (122 acres) of vineyard land that Fèvre owns is of *grand* or *premier cru* classification (he has parcels in six of the seven *grands crus*) and all the wine is aged in new oak for anything up to twelve months. For this grower at least, what the wood treatment does is augment his wines' inherently complex character, as well as lending them even sturdier structure. To some palates, the effect is akin to a previously sylph-like body being pumped up into a muscle-bound monster. To my mind, though, these are in fact mostly successful, perfectly balanced wines. True, they need more time to come into balance than unwooded Chablis, but the bonus is that they age for longer too. Some, notably the *grand cru* Les Clos and the *premier cru* Fourchaume in super-ripe vintages such as 1990, are scarcely distinguishable at first blush from the lusciously honeyed white wines of the Côte d'Or. We are dealing with the same grape variety after all (Chardonnay), and the same region, just about (Burgundy), but the wines are nothing at all like typical Chablis. At their best they are great wines – and yet, tasting them one after another at Fèvre's premises some years ago, I found myself grateful that not all Chablis – or even very much of it – is made in this style. It is essentially the antithesis of what we expect Chablis, even at *cru* level, to taste like. We must hope, perversely, that it doesn't catch on.

An untraditional oaky style that could afford to catch on a bit more is barrel-matured Beaujolais. There is still remarkably little of it about. Certainly, some producers have habitually used large old casks, as opposed to stainless-steel vats, for keeping their wine before release, but these impart no wood flavour to the finished wine (though the slight oxygenation they permit undoubtedly has some very delicately softening effect). Most Beaujolais, even from the better-quality *cru* villages, is released on to the market very young. What retailers will always have in stock, with practically the sole exception of the burlier Moulin-à-Vent, is the most recent vintage. There are unique identifying characteristics in some, perhaps most, of the ten *crus*, but the tendency for a great deal of Beaujolais is always to seem, in Andrew Jefford's term, 'the king of the country wines', in quality far more similar to humble *vin de pays* than an *appellation contrôlée* with its own internal hierarchy. Beaujolais is, for those consumers who can disentangle it from the annual Beaujolais

Nouveau pantomime that so undermines its image, a featherlight red wine with snappy (sometimes aggressively snarling) acidity, no tannin to speak of, and a dead-simple flavour of red fruits such as strawberry or cherry, often with a faintly vulgar edge of cheap confectionery – like pink Opal Fruits or cherry Tunes.

In Fleurie, long held to be one of the best *crus* and the one that commands about the highest prices now on release, a grower called Guy Depardon has pointed the way to what can be made of *cru* Beaujolais, if only its growers would raise their sights a little and forgo some of the handsome profit margin they enjoy from what is essentially a cheap wine to produce. Depardon is the fifth generation of his family to make wine in Fleurie, the vineyard holdings still only amounting to a mere 7.5 hectares (19 acres), plus half a hectare (1.2 acres) in Morgon to the south. He bottles most of his wine between January and March following the harvest, which accords with customary practice in the region, but it is the oak treatment he has given it beforehand that differs from the norm. As well as the basic Fleurie, Depardon makes a Cuvée Prestige, part of which is given a short maturation in oak. In the spring of 1995, I tasted the wines of the most recent vintage in his cellar. The straight Fleurie was astonishing enough. After only one month in the bottle, it was showing a complex bouquet of Fry's Turkish Delight and chocolate on the nose, while the palate was huge, spicy and complex with a roundness and ripeness extraordinary in such a young wine, all deepened by gentle tannin and an unearthly concentration. The Prestige Fleurie was similar on the nose, with crystallised ginger joining the scent of Turkish Delight, while the palate rejoiced in deep, rich, chocolatey concentration. There was a little more tannin, but it was impeccably ripe, and the overall impression was of a forceful, alcoholic, but perfectly integrated red wine.

Depardon then opened a bottle of each wine from the fabled 1991 vintage, one of those improbable years in which the enclave of Beaujolais – virtually alone within France – made classic wines, while everybody else suffered frost wipe-out or harvest-time downpours. The straight Fleurie, here made without filtration of its haze of fermentation deposits in order to capture the full, magisterial intensity of the vintage, offered up a profound nose of coffee and chocolate, backed up by a deep, liquorous plum scent like slivovitz, and then massive concentration of alcoholic plum and black cherry fruit on the palate, with big but controlled tannins and great persistence on the finish. At the time, it tasted as though it needed at least another couple of years to settle down, and it is probably still improving now. The Cuvée Prestige 1991, on the other hand, had snapped shut like a steel trap. It had the structure of Côte de Nuits Pinot Noir on the palate (something like Gevrey-Chambertin), with hints of loganberry and blackberry fruit, but it was essentially completely closed up, set firm in that famous 'dumb' phase fine red wines go into in their middle years. I wondered how long Depardon expected it to take to come round. '*Dix ans?*' he shrugged, reluctant to commit himself too specifically. And this in a region where each year's wines have mostly all been drunk up just as the growers are getting ready to pick the next harvest.

No wines have ever persuaded me more eloquently what the Gamay grape, all but unknown outside Beaujolais and parts of the Loire, may be capable of if given the right handling. Some of that tannic extraction derives from pumping the wine back over its floating cap of pressed grape-skins during the vinification, and some of it derives from low-yielding vines, although the latter point is not crucial since Depardon cheerfully admits that yields for his Fleurie vary hugely, from a fairly conservative 35 hectolitres per hectare (2 tons per acre) to a much more generous 75hl/ha (4.3 tons per acre). What really makes the difference is the barrel-ageing. It is a short process, and the oaked wine is judiciously blended with an equal proportion of unoaked, but as with the best *grand cru* Chablis of William Fèvre, what Guy Depardon has done for his wines by the use of oak is to emphasise and enrich the already existing power and concentration in them. There is better balance in his Fleurie Cuvée Prestige than there is in many a *premier cru* burgundy at considerably higher prices. Country wines these most definitely are not.

On the other hand, Soave – the eternal 'house white' of Italian wine – will never be anything other than a country wine. Neutral in aroma, neutral in flavour, light and forgettable and unimpeachably inoffensive, it was born to be bland. Its colossal annual production pours forth from over-cropping vineyards that, in true Italian fashion, comprise an allegedly distinguished Classico zone surrounded by an extensive ocean of grim anonymity. Just occasionally, a Soave emerges that combines savoury dryness with a momentarily beguiling silkiness of texture. These will be wines produced by growers not hell-bent on squeezing every last millilitre from the vines, and they can be an attractive enough proposition served vigorously chilled with a simple salad, perhaps containing artichokes. However, they are very much the exception that proves the rule.

Growers with land in the Classico area have concentrated on

reducing yields, trying different combinations of the permitted grapes (mainly the ditchwater-dull Trebbiano di Soave and the discomfortingly vegetal Garganega) and essaying practices such as giving the crushed grapes a short maceration on their skins before the alcoholic fermentation begins, a flavour-extraction technique that has paid dividends in parts of southern France where the indigenous grape varieties manage to be more undistinguished than even Trebbiano. In the light of all this, barrique-ageing of Soave seems to have come surprisingly late to the repertoire of conjuring-tricks designed to persuade the wine to taste of something. That this is so perhaps indicates how unlikely such a strategy was to produce sound, balanced wines.

Those producers working with oak always hedge their bets by producing an unwooded, traditional version alongside the barrique-aged releases. This is partly because the investment involved in buying new barrels, and subsequently keeping the wine in storage for longer, means that oak-matured wines are inevitably more expensive. Since nobody expects Soave of all things to be expensive, and the oaked versions have to sit in a producer's range alongside old-school Soave, they must manage to look suitably like premium products. At Ca'Rugate, for example, the Tessari brothers produce a straight Soave Classico, a single-vineyard unoaked Monte Fiorentine and the top-of-the-range barrel-aged Monte Alto. These wines have appreciably higher concentration than the generality, and the oak on the Monte Alto is applied with restraint, so that reasonable balance (and even a certain modest longevity) results. Giuseppe Coffele owns some of the best-sited vineyard land of all, planted on high slopes, from which he offers a straight Classico with a modest hint of orchard fruit to it, as well as the oaky Ca'Visco, of a deeper colour, in which the wood contributes a toffeeish sweetness to the middle palate. Not only does it contain a proportion of barrique-aged wine, but that wine is also nothing other than Chardonnay. It may be a satisfying, commendable wine in itself, but in another way, it could be seen as Soave desperately dolled up with a redeeming dollop of the world's favourite wine. What price regional purity?

Discussions of better-quality Soave, a wine-world parlour game equivalent to coming up with five famous Belgians, usually turn on the name of Leonildo Pieropan, a grower reaching for the Holy Grail of European winemaking – innovative wine that shows due respect to the local conditions (or *terroir*, as the French call them). Harvesting low yields, mixing grapes at differing levels of ripeness to ensure a judicious balance of acidity and richness, and not merely ageing but fermenting the juice in small barriques (always including a proportion of new wood): this is the recipe for his Vigneto La Rocca, an undeniably complex wine in which the oak, intended to play a subtle supporting role, in fact seems very obtrusive when the wine is young, but does harmonise to some extent with time. Then again, considered alongside another single-vineyard wine, the Vigneto Calvarino, it seems a clumsier article. The Calvarino has all the purity of flavour, a mineral austerity just a little enhanced by a fugitive floral note, that low-yielding, concentrated Soave can demonstrate. Even Pieropan's straight Soave Classico Superiore seems a more natural product – assuming such a thing may exist – than the barrel-fermented La Rocca. I am not at all convinced that adding oak to Soave is the way to give it distinction. At best, you create a halfway-house like barrel-aged Entre-deux-Mers; at worst, you end up with a layer of extraneous sweet seasoning on an otherwise characterless, slightly built wine. And there's quite enough of that in the south of France.

If oaked Soave seems an unwieldy proposition, how much more maladroit does oaked German Riesling sound? Possibly no grape variety in the fine wine pantheon is less susceptible to the influence of oak. Its delicacy of constitution in the most illustrious German districts, and the poignant acidity and dazzling aromatic range it can display at all levels from Trocken (fermented-out, bone-dry wines) to Trockenbeerenauslese (the agonisingly concentrated vinous syrup of grapes left to shrivel and rot on the vines) make it undoubtedly the most fascinating variety on the international circuit. None of it needs oak, and yet even here, there are growers unable to resist the temptation to vinify some of their wines in wood. One authority, Tom Stevenson, reckons that as long as Riesling is only fermented in barrel, with little or no actual cask maturation, the resulting wine can be perfectly balanced and successful. If so, I confess I have yet to taste it. Schlossgut Diel in the Nahe is one estate known for its willingness to experiment with oak. Not only Riesling, but Ruländer (the Pinot Gris of France) and others also, are produced as dry, oaky varietals, which in my opinion is about as subtle as spraying on two brands of eau de toilette. Winemaker Armin Diel also produces some exemplary classic Rieslings in vineyards such as Dorsheimer Goldloch, so the fascination with French barriques is all the harder to explain. To a sceptical market, it can only look like an attempt to bestow Gallic sophistication on wines that are, regrettably, hopelessly unpopular.

Exactly what is it, we may wonder, that has made oaky wine such a sure-fire commercial bet? It isn't as though a taste for Meursault-Perrières or Chateau Pichon-Longueville-Lalande at hundreds of pounds a case can have filtered down through the hierarchy of consumption. We may have been weaned on to barrel-aged Rioja Reserva in the 1970s, but who set the precedent for oaky Chardonnay? The answer, like so much else in the contemporary wine world, lies in the southern hemisphere. Alongside the meteoric rise in wine consumption in the UK over the last twenty years, Australian wine has described a similar trajectory. Indeed, the two developments have tracked each other so closely that it is scarcely any exaggeration to say that the wine revolution in Britain was made in Australia. Modulations of taste have occurred along the way, most notably the gradual but measurable shift from white wine to red – but when Australian wine started to be big news in the UK in the 1980s, its flagship product was heavily oaked Chardonnay. Wines such as Penfold's Koonunga Hill Chardonnay and Berri Estates' Chardonnay blazed the trail. They were opulently rich and brimming with summer sun, and to palates that had never come near the pomp and splendour of Le Montrachet, they tasted like nothing else on earth.

The first distinguishing mark of oaked Australian Chardonnay in those days was its vivid yellow colour, often as deep as Tate & Lyle's Golden Syrup. Chardonnay generally produces a fairly pale juice, but as it sits in the cask, it soaks up colour from the wood. It also absorbs the vanillin that is a natural chemical constituent of oak, and if the barrels are brand new, the main olfactory impression will be a strong waft of vanilla. Swirl the wine vigorously, and you would have noticed the viscous trails it left on the inside of the glass. They denoted the high alcohol typical of this style, often approaching a giddy 14% by volume. When tasted, the wine displayed its hot-climate origins in its astonishing degree of residual sugar. Ferocious sun in parts of Australia ripens the grapes to such an extent that they are very high in natural sugars, and thus in potential alcohol. Even when they have finished fermenting, there is often still a perceptible sweetness in the wine, giving it the tongue-coating impact of honey. (Indeed, the general practice in Australia is to add extra tartaric acid, which is naturally present in grape juice, in order to give the wines better balance.) The treatment or 'seasoning' of the oak, when barrels are put together in accordance with the wishes of the winemaker, played a further part. The lightest charring of the insides gave a subtle scent of spent matches or slightly burnt toast. At the extreme end, the wines were acrid with smoke, recalling the sizzling of smoked bacon in the frying-pan. These were, in effect, smoked wines.

This style of wine, in retreat in Australia but still cropping up all over the non-European regions, has since become part of the international language of contemporary winemaking. The only mystery is why it became so popular. It possessed, after all, most of the attributes that discerning drinkers were already thought to have grown out of. This was the very sweetest style of wine that could still technically be called dry and – given the general trend towards dry white wine – it might seem surprising in retrospect that wine of such penetrating sweetness should have attracted such a following. And, just as consumers were supposed to be drinking less but better wine at more tolerable alcohol strengths, here was wine at 13-14%

selling as effortlessly as Export Lager. The truth was, and still is, that the trend towards less alcohol in wine was a complete myth, and the turn from sweet to dry was at best vigorously exaggerated. Oaked Australian Chardonnay was a marketing hit precisely because it was sweet and strong: just the way a whole swathe of the British market has liked its wines ever since we invented port. It was white and it was sweet, like the wine whose previously unchallenged crown it may yet purloin. To the aficionados of the 1980s, Australian Chardonnay was the new Liebfraumilch, only with the added bonus of twice as much alcohol.

Once the taste for strongly oaky wines has been established, it is hard for the palate to adjust back to the subtleties in unoaked or lightly oaked wine. Faced with competition from South Australia, delicate Chardonnays from areas such as the Alto-Adige in northern Italy, or any of the newly emergent former Eastern Bloc countries such as Hungary, were left on the starting-blocks. Thus, at the beginning of the 1990s, it seemed British high-street retailers were falling over themselves to find toasty, charred-tasting, alcoholic Chardonnays wherever they could to feed the insatiable craving created by the Australian revolution. A vin de pays d'Oc Chardonnay might have a delicately singed touch, backed up by modest lemony acidity, but then one tasted the likes of Wolf Blass, Rosemount or Basedow oaked Chardonnays with their clinging, sugary ripeness – a flavour memorably compared by Oz Clarke to pineapple chunks in syrup – and suddenly that seemed like the old-time religion, and the thinner, lighter French wines a vapid imitation. For a while, it looked as though winemakers genuinely had us over a barrel – that there would never be any need to drink an unoaked Chardonnay again.

There was just one problem with this revolution. It didn't come cheap. For a while, Australian Chardonnay was an amazing bargain. These wines weren't of the cheapest, but nor were they prohibitively expensive and, evaluated on the amount of flavour (and alcohol) they delivered per mouthful, they were worth every penny. But oak-ageing is a costly business. A new barrel, coopered and seasoned to a winery's specifications, is a big investment – several hundred pounds' worth, in fact. Moreover, it is only a short-lived asset. After perhaps three uses, the vanilla scent and flavour it can impart noticeably diminishes, and after five, may be hardly there at all. What most wineries do is renew a proportion of their oak each year, so that the barrel-aged Chardonnay in the bottle might be an assemblage of some wine fermented in new oak, a proportion matured in new oak and a proportion matured in used (second- or third-year) oak. Alternatively, for the lighter touch, the wine might be a blend of oaked and completely unoaked lots. Either way, producing a Chardonnay wholly in brand-new oak with every vintage is an option very few can afford. Some buy barrels that have had one or two years' usage from another winery, perhaps one with a sufficiently lofty reputation to make it worth pointing out the provenance to passing journalists, even if not on the labels. (In Muscadet, a fine organic grower called Guy Bossard makes an oaked version of his wine, Cuvée Finement Boisée, in which the juice is fermented in used barrels bought from top burgundy appellations such as Meursault, Chassagne-Montrachet and Pernand-Vergelesses. To emphasise the point, the barrels are depicted on the label.

Strange to say, it is quite a successful wine, the oak adding creaminess, richness and length without obscuring, for those still hankering after textbook Muscadet, its bracingly acid character.)

Notwithstanding such cost-cutting, even cheaper measures had to be found for those producers with neither the means nor the space to keep white wines in barrel for several months. At first, there was a slightly shamefaced air about them, as though the winemakers had been caught doctoring their products with some artificial additive, but as the world has realised just how widespread such practices are, there is greater openness about using them.

The most common is oak chips. Even if you can't afford to put your wine into a whole oak barrel, you can still give it a little wood flavour by infusing it with some chopped-up oak. Chips may be immersed in the juice before fermentation or added once it has started, when the temperature generated helps to maximise the take-up of flavour from the relatively smaller, and more inconstant, contact they offer. The process is subject to all the variables that apply to barrels, from the type of oak used to the degree of toasting, but in the case of top-quality French wood such as Limousin can be as little as 5% of the cost of having bespoke barrels made. Some producers use a mixture of the two techniques, supplementing the declining flavour of third- or fourth-year wood by dunking some chips in the wine as well.

The salient question for the consumer, then, becomes: is a chipped wine inferior to a barrel-aged wine? To some commentators, the answer is undoubtedly yes. There is some evidence that wine made exclusively with oak chips can be subject to higher levels of volatile acidity. That may mean it could develop vinegary off-flavours after a much shorter time in your wine-rack than barrel-aged wine, meaning that these are not wines for keeping. Then there is the more general point that barrel-ageing, after all, does more for a wine than simply give it an oaky flavour. Minuscule quantities of air seep through the pores in the wood while a wine is maturing, allowing it to breathe and imparting a softer, more complex feel. A wine sitting in a stainless-steel vat with a bag of chips suspended in it does not benefit from this effect, but merely takes up the wood flavour in a more cosmetic way.

So how do you tell if an oaky wine has been chipped or not? You don't. At least, the producer isn't keen to tell you on the label and, for the time being (and wrongly), is not legally required to. It may nonetheless be quite obvious in two other ways. Firstly, an oaky wine selling at £3.99 is not very likely to have been matured in barrels. The cost of barrel maturation has to be recouped through the asking price and, unless the winery has sufficient wherewithal to produce a loss-leading cheapie to support the top-dollar premium wine, a toasty-tasting Chardonnay is quite likely to have been chipped. More tellingly still, if the back-label refers simply to 'a flavour of peaches, butter and oak' or describes the wine as 'ripe and fruity, and with subtle oak influence', it is almost inevitable that some sort of barrel substitute is being referred to. Almost invariably, if a producer has invested in barrels, he or she will want to tell you precisely where they came from, what percentage were new, and how long the wine spent in them. Basically, if you don't see the word 'barrels' or one of its synonyms – casks, hogsheads, puncheons – you are likely to be feasting on chips.

Then again, for the thrift-conscious winery, a bag of chips is not the only diet. The next development was barrel inserts. This was intended as a step up from the chip-bag. Introducing staves of new oak into a used and inert barrel has the advantage of allowing the wine the oxygenating effect of sitting in a barrel, at the same time as it is imbued with some new oak flavour from whole staves, and it is of course cheaper than using whole new barrels. Whether the stave technique produces a significantly more convincing result than the bag of chips, however, is a moot point.

At the murkier depths, some producers have (often illegally) resorted to adding oak flavouring to their wines, in the form of wood extract. Not merely vanillary oak flavour can be added in this way, but a degree of tannic extract may also be present, handy for beefing up a feeble red. Or a drop of vanilla essence may be added at concentrations of no more than one ten-thousandth by volume – just sufficient to add flavour without being detectable as a crude additive. Oak extract is also available in powdered form, but is fiddlier to manage because it carries the risk of clouding the wine. Needless to say, wines that have been adulterated in this way have even less chance of living healthily through lengthy bottle storage than those that have been chipped or staved.

It is not my intention to suggest that the world of wine would be anything other than poorer if the use of oak were suddenly found to be hazardous to health and abolished overnight by European Union diktat. Who doesn't prefer the richer cask-aged Rioja to the fruitily simple *sin crianza* version? Who wouldn't want Puligny-Montrachet if offered the choice between that and unoaked St-Véran? But these are not the only choices to be made. Do we want unoaked New

Zealand Sauvignon Blanc, with its cascade of bright, jolly fruit flavours, or do we want California barrel-fermented Fumé Blanc, a fundamentally misconceived wine made in clumsy imitation of (oak-free) Pouilly-Fumé? Would we prefer a richly musky Alsace Pinot Gris or a barrel-matured Ruländer from Germany's oak innovators? In each case I heartily opt for the former. Although oak is a wonderful thing, there is undoubtedly too much of it about these days, particularly in white wines, whether in the form of actual barrels or one of the inexpensive short-cut methods. It is in those short-cut wines that one especially resents it. The impulse is nothing other than a cynical attempt to add a layer of complexity the wine doesn't intrinsically possess. It is in no sense an attempt to incorporate the savoury depth of oak influence as an integral element, but is being imposed against the grain of the wine, as it were, as a quick route to opulent richness, and whether the wine requires it or not. An analogy is the over-use of smoking in speciality food products, in which the original article – be it an almond, a scallop or a young cheese – surrenders its original flavour to the acrid tang of wood smoke. Here, too, there are shortcuts, so that the smoke may well have been sprayed on as an essence, rather than absorbed from smouldering embers. In the end, there are only a limited number of uses for smoked garlic or smoked tomatoes, and smoked Chardonnay was a flavour that palled almost as quickly.

There is, anyway, evidence of many winemakers taking on board the notion that it is possible to have too much of a good thing. Although it is still in plentiful evidence down under, Australian Chardonnay is much less in thrall to the flavour of oak than it was fifteen years ago. Where a winemaker offers the market an unoaked and an oaked cuvée, the latter at a reasonably higher price, the barrel-aged version is often only a shade richer and fuller than the first, which at least means the unoaked style doesn't have to go into the world as the poor man's option, the bottle you only buy if you haven't got the extra quid for the better one. Ultimately, with Chardonnay particularly, it takes more winemaking skill and more imagination to produce a complex, interesting, ageworthy wine without barrels than with. But wherever we find this skill in abundance – among the best Chablis growers, among Rieslings, Sauvignons and Chenin Blanc wines the world over, among the aromatic varietal wines of Alsace – we should celebrate it. As I said in the last chapter, uniformity is what will kill the wine renaissance. It doesn't always have to be Chardonnay. And it doesn't have to be chips with everything.

Chapter 6

DRINKING STARS

Or: How the sparkling wine industry got itself into a froth

THE INVENTION OF SPARKLING WINE in the northern French district of Champagne – in its mawkishly sentimental version – is one of the great enduring myths of wine history. Believed implicitly for over 200 years, it told of how a blind monk, one Dom Pérignon, treasurer and cellarmaster of the abbey at Hautvillers in the early eighteenth century, came to taste his newly-made wine one day. The traditional wines of Champagne were thin, still, acidic creations, fit only for drinking early, but on this particular day a little Disneyesque stardust must have been sprinkled in the air, because the old man was in for a world-changing surprise. Instead of the usual flat, simple wine, he found an exotic new substance cascading over his tongue, effervescing in little rills and bursting all over his palate with a thousand tiny detonations.

Tremulous with excitement, he is said to have cried out in his joy, 'Come quickly, brothers! I am drinking stars!'

The rest, of course, is history. And history, as Henry Ford told us, is bunk.

We have an abiding need to believe in myths of origin. There is a roadside inn in France that claims to be the world's first ever restaurant. Somebody somewhere, no doubt, lays claim to being the first person ever to wear a baseball cap back to front. But in the last 25 years or so, a number of studies has shown that, whatever Pérignon's contribution to the development of the wines of Champagne (and it certainly appears to have involved the refinement of clarification techniques, as well as pioneering the production of white wines wholly or partly from red grape varieties, now standard practice in the sparkling wine industry world-wide), it did not involve the discovery, invention or even divine transubstantiation of the fizzy drink now known as champagne. In this respect Nicholas Faith's *The Story of Champagne* (1988) was a milestone, and others have since developed and extended his research. Nobody invented champagne, whatever the song says.

Fizzy wine – however much it might seem like a one-off idea – just happened, and was happening, latest research suggests, as long ago as Roman times. Fizziness was a long-recognised fault that could overcome a chemically unstable wine in the period before stabilisation was understood, long before Louis Pasteur. It was a particular hazard in the severe winters of France's northernmost wine district, when temperatures might drop to a level at which yeasts in the wine were unable to complete the work of fermentation. The wine would sit dormant in the cask until the first warmer weather of the following spring, whereupon the yeasts would awaken from their enforced hibernation and carry on consuming what sugar remained in it. With further fermentation came further carbon dioxide, resulting in a wine that had bubbles in it when the cask was tapped.

Bubbly wine was a disaster. One very occasionally comes across it now. In a young wine that has only been recently bottled, bubbles are not considered a fault; technically it is referred to as youthful spritziness. It will disperse with time, and while it is there, may be thought to confer a certain refreshing vivacity. Youthful Muscadet *sur lie* often has it. On the other hand, an older bottle that has been cellared for a few years, perhaps at temperatures a little higher than the optimum, and that also turns out to be slightly fizzy when tasted, is most definitely spoiled. Insufficiently stabilised before bottling, it is now re-fermenting. One can only heave a sigh, and throw it away, which would have been pretty much the educated response to fizzy wine in the cellars at Hautvillers when Dom Pérignon ruled the roost. Before champagne as a deliberately sparkling wine had caught on, there had been no need for the reinforced bottles now universally used. When the wine had been bottled, therefore, the hazard was even greater. Explosions in the cellar were commonplace, with a significant risk of injury in disturbing a bottle that had quietly fizzed itself into a tumult. Against such a background, it is possible to imagine what an unlikely commercial proposition an intentionally eruptive, bubbling wine once was.

In fact, as Tom Stevenson has shown in Christie's *World Encyclopedia of Champagne and Sparkling Wine* (1998), the practice of adding more sugar to a wine in order to provoke a re-fermentation was already established in England before Pérignon had even been appointed at Hautvillers. A paper unearthed from the archives of the Royal Society has removed the last prop from the myth of champagne's invention. Entitled 'Some Observations concerning the Ordering of Wines', it was written by one Christopher Merret, and given to a convocation of the newly formed scientific research society in December 1662. 'Our wine coopers of later times,' he writes, 'use vast quantities of sugar and molasses to all sorts of wines to make them drink brisk and sparkling, and to give them spirit as also to mend their bad taste.' At a stroke, this solved the mystery previously posed by the tantalising reference to such a drink in a Restoration drama by Sir George Etherege – *The Man of Mode*, written in 1676 – to 'sparkling Champaign', a drink credited with aphrodisiac properties (albeit short-lived ones):

It quickly recovers

Poor languishing lovers,

Makes us frolic and gay, and drowns all sorrow;

But, Alas, we relapse again on the morrow.

Whereas contemporary French documentation refers to the systematic production of champagne as only having emerged in the 1690s, here, some twenty years earlier, is a reference not merely to a sparkling wine, but specifically to sparkling 'Champaign'. Merret's Royal Society paper is now the earliest written account we have of the vinification procedure that was to become known as the *méthode champenoise*.

In 1728, a law was enacted by the French court that permitted the shipment of the wines of Champagne in bottles, rather than in the bulk casks in which they had previously had to be transported.

Scarcely more than a year later, and less than fifteen years after Dom Pérignon's death, the first house to be devoted to producing sparkling Champagne wines, Ruinart, was established in Reims. The taste for sparkling champagne was soon to spread far and wide. It eventually found immense favour in the nineteenth century with the Romanovs, the Tsarist dynasty in Russia, who preferred it to taste luxuriously sweet, more syrupy indeed than the modern-day fizzy wine of Asti. By then, its origins as a makeshift way of adding vigour to a dull white wine had been long forgotten. The high prices it sold for (and it is worth remembering that it used to be stratospherically more expensive in relation to average incomes than it is now) meant it wove around itself an aura of opulent mystique that winemakers in other regions could only gape in envy at. Arguably no other winemaking innovation since, not even the perfecting of the various classic styles of fortified wine, has since had such an impact on the market as did the discovery of how to give a wine controlled effervescence. The fashion for sweet wines comes and goes; the commercial favour of products like madeira, marsala and Málaga seems to be going, going, gone, but champagne is abidingly popular. So chic and so sought-after is it, indeed, that even those who don't particularly like it tell themselves they do. This is the kind of market profile beyond the combined pecuniary might of every PR company in the Western world to create: a product that effortlessly sells itself. Not even Solomon in all his glory was arrayed like a bottle of fizz in an ice-bucket, cork drawn and chilled to a nicety, waiting to fill those long, thin glasses with a golden (or salmon-pink) flurry of activity.

Somehow, though, the champagne producers have managed in

recent years to dig their own collective grave. During the economic boom years of the 1980s, consumption of the product rocketed, in the UK particularly. Two huge successive vintages in 1982 and 1983 helped to deflate its price and, suddenly, where once it had been relegated to some hallowed shelf in the wine-shop, it now found itself the subject of pile-it-high special offers. The Seagram company's retail chain Oddbins led the way. Listing dozens of brands, rather than just four or five of the famous names, Oddbins made champagne-buying fun, and they made it democratic. The supermarkets weighed in alongside with their own, sometimes loss-leading, brands, selling for ruthlessly competitive prices. J. Sainsbury sold an excellent blanc de blancs at £9.99 for what felt like years. Champagne ceased to be a special-occasion wine and became a weekend apéritif, even a what-the-hell Tuesday night pick-me-up after a godawful day at the office. It slithered down the social scale hand-in-hand with smoked salmon, slumming it in the sticky mitts of Essex boys earning telephone-number salaries on the Futures Exchange, being measured out by the glass at effervescing profit margins in half-smart city bars. At Kettners in Soho, flagship branch of the Pizza Express chain, the champagne bar listed even more brands and vintages than Oddbins, at sufficiently modest mark-ups to ensure the place was banged out every night.

No market can expand indefinitely of course, as American stock-market investors discovered in 1929, and champagne's bubbles were about to burst in a very big way with the coming of the vicious recession of the early 1990s. Even beforehand, though, the end of the boom was being engineered in the most unlikely quarter of all – Epernay, administrative headquarters of the champagne industry. Although in the immediate aftermath it came to be much denied, a view gradually germinated among those charged with overseeing the product's image, the CIVC (Comité Interprofessionel du Vin de Champagne), that the wine was suffering from its new-found popularity. If it ceased to be the wine of celebration and special occasions, was it not in danger of surrendering its enviable niche position? If it was trickling into the mouths of the huddled masses, previously used to encountering it only at christenings, what had they to aspire or look up to? Just as some reactionary old twit famously said that youth was too good to be wasted on the young, champagne, it seemed, was too good to be wasted on those who wanted to drink it. The CIVC later emphasised that this was never their official view. Nevertheless, prices began to go up. Between 1989 and 1990, the British retail price of a bottle of non-vintage grande marque champagne increased by an average of £2, having previously taken three years to put on 50p. Moreover, quality was taking a nosedive, as certain houses had begun releasing their vintage wines at barely four years old, disingenuously suggesting that, where previously they had been intended to gain complexity by ageing on their yeast deposits in the cellars of Champagne, now it was up to the consumer to mature them at home. An acrimonious debate ensued over the rights and wrongs of it all, at the height of which Oz Clarke conducted a tasting for his annual wine guide of sparkling wines from other regions under the rubric, 'Who needs champagne?' For this misdemeanour, he was blackballed by the Champagne Bureau in London, and forbidden from attending champagne events or tastings until a sufficiently contrite recantation was forthcoming. Other writers in turn announced that they would not write about champagne until the *fatwa* was lifted. The industry had scored a wickedly curling, in-off own-goal.

As tempers cooled during the 1990s, the industry regrouped and committed itself to a new quality charter that, among other points, lengthened the minimum maturation time on yeast for the non-vintage wines, as well as, significantly, eliminating the inferior second pressing of the grapes (the *deuxième taille*) that was responsible for the rough, coarse flavours in many of the cheaper wines. To compound the whole spring-cleaning exercise, prices stabilised, and even dropped a little, as the houses realised that commercial goodwill was too precious an asset to be squandered.

But not long after the press had been at one in welcoming the industry's acceptance of criticism and in congratulating the *champenois* on three gloriously successful, and intriguingly different, vintage releases in 1988, 1989 and 1990, the CIVC once again shot itself in the foot. It was announced that there was likely to be a shortage of champagne as demand increased in the run-up to the millennium celebrations. Buy now, was the message, or risk having to drink something inferior on the great night. When it was pointed out that much of the non-vintage champagne that would be on sale in the latter part of 1999 hadn't even been made yet, the shrill communiqué was toned down: now it said there would only be a shortage of the vintage wines. Several of the more conscientious houses then revealed that the cellars of Reims and Epernay were awash with stocks. In a startlingly obvious marketing strategy, most houses had held back stocks precisely to meet the high demand of December 1999. There would be plenty to go round.

In any case, by the end of the 1980s, the world had changed forever. It was from this time that the quality of sparkling wines from other parts of the world at last began to be taken seriously. There had always been other sparklers with reputations of their own. Above the grisly likes of branded *vin mousseux* and frothing, screw-top Lambrusco in every colour of the vinous rainbow, there was Spanish cava, and indeed other French wines such as sparkling Saumur from the Loire, Crémant de Bourgogne and the less widely available but generally better Crémant d'Alsace. And there was always dear old Asti, rid since 1993 of that horrible S-word that for so many years had always made it sound so – well, *spewy* (not to mention an unhappy assonance with 'diamante', so that a refreshing, grape-sweet sparkler had been stuck with a name unhelpfully hesitating between imitation gemstones and vomit). Some of these wines could be very variable indeed – for my money, Spanish cava deserved the accolade for Greatest Benefit of the Doubt Given, for all that it has always been made by the champagne method – while others were soundly reliable. (Poor-quality Asti is as rare as hen's teeth.) But now, coming up on the inside track, other sparkling wines were appearing made in the precise image of champagne itself, using the same method and often the same grape varieties, and selling for a fraction of the price. As the wine press started giving them serious coverage, sections of the champagne industry were inclined to dismiss them as lacking the finesse of *la vraie chose*, but the truth was that the writing was on the wall, and many of the more forward-looking houses had already seen it.

If the world was turning to Chardonnay and Cabernet Sauvignon wines from the southern hemisphere as enthusiastically as it seemed, would it not be long before it investigated what these countries had to offer in the way of fizz? Moët et Chandon, still in many consumers' minds the brand most emblematically representative of champagne, led the way. Back in 1973, long before New World wines had made any significant impact in Europe, Moët bought a tract of land in the Napa Valley, California, a region now basking in international recognition as the source of outstanding wines in all styles. This was to be the modern vinous equivalent of the start of the Gold Rush. Nearly thirty years later California remains the number one target for overseas investment by the champagne industry, and Moët's initiative has since been followed by Deutz, Louis Roederer, G.H. Mumm, Piper-Heidsieck, Pommery, Taittinger and Laurent-Perrier. Some of these enterprises, such as Mumm's involvement in Cuvée Napa and Laurent-Perrier's with Iron Horse Vineyards in Sonoma County, are joint-venture agreements. Others, like Roederer's Quartet and Moët's own Domaine Chandon, are go-it-alone operations, intended to compete with the local sparkling wine scene on its own terms. What is clear, as more of these diversifications come on stream, is that for those producers involved, they represent a kind of insurance policy against leaner economic times, to which champagne is naturally very sensitive. In addition, though, they have enabled the industry to gain a commercial foothold in the sector of the market that would baulk at spending over £20 on a bottle of fizz for the weekend, but might happily buy one at under £12.

Finding growing sites sufficiently cool to be conducive to the production of quality sparkling wine has proved more difficult in Australia, where the climate is much less forgiving than on the breezy California coast. Nonetheless, Moët picked out one of the less torrid districts in Victoria, the Yarra Valley, for its Green Point fizz, which has now turned out to be one of the most elegantly graceful sparklers in Australia. New Zealand has a much cooler climate, being considerably closer to the Antarctic Circle, which is why the highly regarded Cloudy Bay winery – which produces a rich and distinguished sparkling wine called Pelorus – has attracted investment from Veuve Clicquot, and why Deutz chose the South Island for its Marlborough Cuvée, which has the unmistakably crisp, vivacious style of good young champagne.

Moreover, it isn't only the New World countries that have been the focus of attention. Moët (yes, them again) have established a facility in Penedés, the heart of Spain's cava production. Cava was for a long time only of very patchy quality but had occupied a modest corner of the market for those who wanted a dry sparkler at a gentler price than champagne. Given its method of production, it always had the potential to be a lot better than it actually was, and in recent years winemaking improvements have begun to transform it. With its Torre del Gall wine, Moët has been perfectly poised to take advantage of this renaissance.

It hasn't all been plain sailing. Undoubtedly, mistakes were made in the 1980s when some of the California wines suffered from overproduction in the vineyards, leading to some vapid, flavourless sparklers. Virtually all of the world's best wines, including sparkling, are produced from low-yielding vines, and the soils of the Napa Valley, being immensely rich and fertile, can militate against quality if the vineyards are not subjected to careful husbandry. The balance has now largely been redressed, though, and plenty of refined and complex wines are now emerging.

As the external ventures of the champagne industry have come to prominence in the last few years, there have been whispers of a new conspiracy theory. This insisted that no serious champagne house would want to cut its own throat by making equally good wines elsewhere for lower prices, and so they were bound to cut corners on quality with their Californian and Australian offerings, in order to preserve the aura of elitism around the original product, as well as to justify its premium. Perhaps this suggestion was the last residue of the vitriol that flowed during the debates of 1990, but in any case, there is nothing in it. If the quality of any wine with a particular producer's name on it were seen to be less than reliable, it would eventually have a concomitant effect on that company's other products, including champagne itself. Meanwhile the price differential is slowly but surely closing, as world sparkling wine production approaches 2.3 billion bottles a year, of which champagne is only 12%. Some New World sparkling wines are now as expensive as the less well-known champagnes now, and if they continue to gain ascendancy in the market, as there is every indication, the trend can only continue. If it has often been said that it took the Australians to produce palatable wines in the south of France, perhaps – conversely – it has taken the *champenois* to help the New Worlders make great bubbly.

Champagne is essentially an artificial construct. Where most other viniculture involves growing and ripening a season's grapes, fermenting them, ageing the wine (or not) and releasing it, champagne is the product of a whole series of interventionist measures. The vast majority is blended from different vintages. Once a base wine has been made, it has a slug of sugar solution (*liqueur de tirage*) added in order to start up a second fermentation in the bottle. That second-ary fermentation produces a deposit of dead yeast cells that has to be painstakingly worked up to the top of the bottle (either by hand or machine) and then removed. Just before the cork is put in, a final ingredient (*liqueur d'expédition*) is added, in order to determine the overall level of sweetness or otherwise in the finished wine. All sorts of variations on the basic recipe have been essayed over the generations, and some styles have stuck. There is vintage wine, the product of a single, theoretically finer harvest, which always sells at a considerably higher margin than non-vintage. Good vintage cham-pagne (the 1995 looks like being a star) needs to be drunk at something approaching ten years old to show at its best. A wine made entirely from Chardonnay is known as blanc de blancs, and is intended to be a lighter style than the normal blend of red and white, but this whiter-than-white style too can take on a beguiling, toasty richness as it ages. A white wine made solely from the region's red grapes (Pinot Noir and Pinot Meunier) is labelled blanc de noirs. This, more than any other offering of the industry, may be considered a true homage to Dom Pérignon, the man who per-fected the methodology for producing a clear white wine from grapes with red skins. A slightly sweet wine is labelled Demi-Sec, a distinctly sweet one Doux, the two styles created at the last moment of the process by adding a dosage of sugar solution with more sugar in it than goes into the standard bone-dry, or Brut, version. A wine that is just a shade less dry than Brut, but not as sweet as Demi-Sec, is labelled Sec. One a little sweeter than Sec, but drier than Brut, is labelled Extra Dry, while at the other end, a wine labelled Rich is even sweeter than Doux. Wines that are kept on the yeast sediments for much longer than average to gain extra complexity, and then have it removed just prior to commercial release, are known as RD (recently disgorged, or *récemment dégorgé*, if you prefer). At the top of the tree are the various houses' premium products, the *cuvées prestiges* or *cuvées de luxe*, wines that may come in extraordinarily pretentious packaging at prices to induce a blackout, but also, if properly aged and respectfully served, occasionally demonstrate what all the fuss is about.

All but one of these variations on a basic theme may pass everyday consumers by; the exception is likely to be pink. Rosé champagne itself can be either vintage or non-vintage (some houses make both, most one or the other), but to a buyer seeking to ring the changes, pink seems the obvious one to go for. That said, pink champagne is one of those commodities, like white chocolate or Boyzone, that nobody will publicly admit to liking. In the industry itself, it is considered a *vin de frivolité* – or worse, if we are to believe Nicholas Faith. In *The Story of Champagne*, he declares on behalf of the naturally more reticent *champenois*: 'They have always hated it'. If so, it is hard to see why. Commercially, rosé is pretty good news. While certainly subject to the vagaries of fashion, its sales are increasing year on year. In 1999 just over a million bottles were sold in the UK – a 21% rise on the previous year. As recently as 1981, annual British sales of rosé were a mere 90,000 bottles, although admittedly that was in the midst of severe recession. Even if all the Valentine's Day and Mothering Sunday sales are subtracted from the equation, somebody is drinking it. Furthermore, whatever the champagne houses themselves say on the matter, surprisingly few of the big names decline to produce a rosé. Some – Pol Roger, Veuve Clicquot and Bollinger among them – sell only a vintage-dated pink, scarcely the strategy of houses pandering to the vulgar end of the market.

Notwithstanding its impressive prominence, rosé champagne could be an even healthier commercial proposition if only there weren't such a shaming price differential. There is in fact no economic reason for most of the pink wines to be any dearer than the whites. The exceptions would be those wines that have been *saigné*, in other words, macerated, to achieve the colour. Staining the white juice pink by means of a short infusion of the red grapeskins is a relatively tricky procedure. Not only does it depend on judging each vat to a tee, but the degree of pigmentation obtainable from the thin-skinned Pinot Noir variety is acutely vintage-sensitive, and no standard formula can be applied from year to year. Moreover, some colour loss during the secondary bottle fermentation must be allowed for, although the precise degree inevitably remains unpredictable. These factors together account for the significant colour variation from bottle to bottle in those rosés (including Laurent-Perrier, Daniel Dumont and Vollereaux) still made by maceration.

When a wine is being produced to an allegedly consistent house style, as non-vintage champagne is intended to be, colour variation sounds like a marketing manager's nightmare. Thus it is that, since pink fizz was introduced 200 years ago, various methods of corner-cutting have been resorted to, all taking the form of additives rather than a vinification method. In the early nineteenth century an infusion of elderberries in cream of tartar was the preferred colouring agent, and was found noxious enough to be superseded within a generation by cochineal, the livid red exudation of crushed Mexican beetles, since indispensable to cooks making pink frosting for fairy-cakes. Then cheaper, synthetic dyes had their day, until someone finally had the bright idea of adding a slug of red wine to the bottle. By the time the *appellation contrôlée* system was formulated, adding finished wine to champagne to colour it was sufficiently established as a technique to be incorporated into the regulations. Champagne remains, anomalously, the only example of an AC in the whole of French wine law to permit such a practice. No still rosé wine is allowed the luxury of such a short cut. Unsurprisingly, though, this is how fully 98% of all pink champagne is nowadays given its colour.

If you are not going to make it properly, the customer might object, why make it at all? The answer, perhaps, is that because macerated pink champagnes could justifiably sell for a higher premium, the wine-coloured ones may as well rake in the extra too, even though they are distinctly less labour-intensive to make. The time is clearly overdue for the CIVC to require rosé producers to state on the label the method used. Since we can safely assume this will meet with apoplexy from most of the houses, the next best thing would be for the maceration producers voluntarily to state their method on the label, leaving consumers to draw their own conclusions about the rest.

What, then, do we expect of pink champagnes, compared to their white counterparts? The first and most obvious point is colour. These can be disarmingly pretty wines that come into their own for outdoor summer drinking. There is an extraordinarily broad colour spectrum, from onion-skin tawny to the faintest blush, from delicate coral or the pink of poached salmon (probably the most attractive shade) to full-blown shocking Schiaparelli. The standard addition of red wine, Coteaux Champenois rouge, is 10-15% of the bottle's contents, the darker ones obviously at the upper end of that span. There has to be more to a wine than mere colour, though, and what is hoped for above all is a scent and flavour of red fruits – cherries, perhaps, or, classically, strawberries. Given that young Pinot Noir so often has this attribute, it is hard to see why so much rosé champagne should be devoid of fruit, indistinguishable on the nose and palate from the white wines. Sometimes, on the other hand, there is a distinct aroma of rough young red wine. Only rarely, though, does that basket of summer strawberries come wafting up. (Pol Roger's heaven-scented 1982 vintage was a shatteringly beautiful example. Their 1993 goes some way to approximating it.) Some houses, most notably Ruinart, balance the proportion of red wine by making up the blend with Chardonnay. Their late-release 1988 rosé is a highly accomplished exemplar, for all that it may seem to possess a peculiar density of texture hardly ever encountered in sparkling wine. It is also the exception to the rule that older vintage rosé is seldom worth drinking. Young and fresh tends to be the yardstick for drinking these wines.

Informative labelling, more honest pricing and more dependable fruitiness would go a long way to improving the take-up of this category, but it is always likely to be handicapped for as long as it is seen as hopelessly gender-specific. A gang of lads out on a jolly is not likely to be tempted by the prospect of pink champers all round. Then again, if the Bordeaux producers can overcome their innate conservatism and sell claret, as they did in 1999, with an ad campaign touting it as the next best sex-aid after ice-cream, surely the *champenois* might see a killing to be made with sparkling pink in the gay market?

Champagne's principal rivals now come from the southern hemisphere, and, to a lesser extent, California. Blind tastings, including those carried out annually at the International Wine Challenge, confirm the emergence of the so-called New World countries. Australia does particularly well, but there are also good wines from New Zealand and, increasingly, South Africa. Australia is helped by a style of fizz it has made all its own: sparkling red wines made from Shiraz or Cabernet Sauvignon. At first, these wines are quite startling, especially if they have been fermented out to dryness. Astringent tannin and roaring alcohol levels (one producer makes a sparkling Grenache at 14.5% alcohol) are very unusual and, in a sense, rather cumbersome qualities to encounter in a sparkler. Clearly, we have left the notion of an appetising apéritif far behind. With some residual sugar in them, though, they can be idiosyncratically charming wines, with the mouth-coating blackcurrant ripeness of effervescent Ribena. South Africa's fizz producers, meanwhile, have largely gone for extended yeast-ageing, whereby the wines acquire a lush, creamy texture and complexity of flavour in a process known as autolysis. Graham Beck, Pongracz and Pierre Jourdan are all good. In New Zealand, crispness and vivacity are all, the cool climate reliably reproducing the vagaries of Champagne itself (look for Pelorus from Cloudy Bay or Deutz Marlborough Cuvée), while in California, arguably more dedicated than any other non-European region to the assiduous theoretical study of viticulture and vinification, constant improvements in winery practice are beginning to pay handsome dividends. Try Domaine Chandon, Roederer Quartet or Cuvée Napa. Snapping at their heels are wines from the European backwaters. Franciacorta in the Lombardia region of northern Italy should soon be a serious contender in international circles, having been deservedly elevated to DOCG status for its sparkling wines, while the cava producers of Spain, we continue to hope, will one day show us unequivocally what they are made of (Parellada and Macabeo, mostly, with judicious admixtures of Chardonnay cropping up in the swishest bottles). Even little old England may one day turn out some sparkling wine worthy of its price.

Which, then, of all these regions is best poised to knock the old stager, champagne, off its pedestal once and for all?

The answer is . . . none of them. Whilst I am no stranger to iconoclasm in wine matters, and for all that the greed and hypocrisy rife throughout the champagne industry gives me more virulent heartburn than a rush-released young blanc de blancs, I cannot obscure the truth. Champagne is the greatest sparkling wine on the planet. Its finest productions (not always its most expensive) are so indisputably and entirely in another class that direct comparisons with other sparkling wines are almost always grotesquely unfair on the latter. Blind tastings do indeed confirm that fine sparkling wines are being made in other regions, but also that they are simply not as good as champagne. Others may claim not to revere champagne to this degree, but their pronouncements are invariably belied once the serious work of comparative evaluation begins.

At the 1999 Wine Challenge, fifteen gold medals were awarded to white and rosé sparkling wines. Of those, fourteen were to champagnes (vintage and non-vintage), with the interloper being

Champagne Roederer's California offering, Quartet. Among silver medallists, of which there were 52, no fewer than 41 were champagne, the balance being made up of five Australian wines, three from New Zealand, and one each from South Africa, Italy and the Loire. Adding in Australia's sparkling reds (not a category the *champenois* deem a particular threat to their ascendancy) augmented that country's tally by one gold and two silvers. In the Rosé category, both of the golds and all seven of the silvers were champagnes, while in the medium-to-sweet section, which produced no golds, both of the silvers were champagnes. If this is the stiffest competition champagne ever faces (and results like these are reliably replicated every year at the Wine Challenge, even though there is no shortage of non-champagne sparklers submitted), the industry must wonder what it has to worry about.

What it has to worry about, if anything, is that such results do not straightforwardly reflect patterns of consumption. A sparkling Chenin Blanc from the Loire costing about £4.50 is always likely to find more takers, assuming anybody knows it exists, than the basic non-vintage champagne at £20-plus. But if the argument is about pure quality, about such ineffable matters as balance, finesse, complexity, length and longevity, then champagne continues to have the game all its own way, notwithstanding its investments overseas. It might be fairer to taste the other wines in their own categories, as happens to some degree at the Challenge and more rigorously at other tastings, but that of course would be to acknowledge even more bluntly that the comparison is between chalk and cheese. It isn't that chalk can't be compared with cheese. It's just that chalk doesn't taste as nice.

The reasons for this indestructible preference lie, as they always do in wine, in issues like viticulture and climate. Champagne is grown on poor chalky soils at the virtual margins of where the vine will flourish. It isn't that sparkling wines can't successfully be pro- duced in hotter climates, and even, as many Australian wines have demonstrated, by other methods of vinification. It is more a ques- tion of what sort of balance we expect to find in the wine in the glass. The finest sparkling wines are produced from a light, acidic base wine of relatively neutral character and low alcohol. These wines may not have much going for them as they are – as was decid- edly felt by those Londoners who, 350 years ago, first added sugar to jazz them up a bit – but as such, with the right treatments, they result in sparkling wines that have the right weight in the mouth once they have put on more alcohol after the second fermentation, and that have the acidity to sustain ageing in either the region's cel- lars or your own. A sparkling wine that tastes of ripe mango and doesn't have that brittle edge to it may be a perfectly palatable drink, but it is never going to be as serious a wine.

For the time being and for the foreseeable future, then, we are stuck with champagne as the best game in town. The antics of the producers, resorting to litigation at the drop of a hat in order to stop any other commodity (even perfume) from using the name, may leave us cold. Their product may frustrate and exasperate us unduly when the quality is poor, because the outlay has been so steep (for precisely this reason, Jancis Robinson has correctly said that cheap champagne is the worst-value wine in the world), but we seem to continue taking the risk. In doing so, we can at least console our- selves that non-vintage champagne is cheaper than classed-growth

Bordeaux or *grand cru* burgundy, other wines that are not expected to form part of our everyday diet. We can also confidently anticipate that no sparkling-wine experience on earth will come close to that of fully mature vintage champagne. And when all is said and drunk, what do you really want to be opening on New Year's Eve? Sparkling Loire Chenin? A cheeky little bubbly from Mudgee? Brownish-pink cava rosado with a scent of horseradish?

Thought not.

Chapter 7

WOULD YOU LIKE TO SEE THE LIST?

Or: Why are restaurants still getting wine so wrong?

NOWHERE IS IT WORTH TRYING more to match food and wine correctly than in the restaurant. With the exception of that mercifully short-lived moment in the early 1990s when business lunchers with an afternoon's currency speculation ahead of them began to follow the American habit of having mineral water to drink, most people eating out prefer to enjoy at least a glass of something to go with their food – and perhaps a glass of something to precede it as well. Most, on being offered an apéritif, also still seem to pursue the safer option of a standard bar drink: a spirit and mixer or a glass of house white, less often a glass of house champagne, less often still a tot of dry sherry. But with the exception of the first, these are choices surprisingly fraught with peril, even now.

Wine by the glass is a facility that restaurants, pubs and wine bars have long been enjoined to offer. It's a good idea, not only for those wishing to drink less than a bottle, or desiring a small amount of something else to go with a specific course before (or, more rarely, after) the main wine is to be drunk, but also as an apéritif. For some reason, though, it is a phenomenon that still sits very uneasily with British catering. Certainly, the amount of wastage engendered is not to be taken lightly, particularly if a range of wines by the glass is being offered at more or less the same price. But the tetchiness encountered in pubs serving food – and even in fairly serious restaurants – if one has to send back a glass of wine, because the bottle has been opened and resealed so often that the contents are well on the way to acetification (vinegarising), is tiresome indeed. Some establishments use the vacuum-pump device to extract corrosive oxygen from the bottle. Others simply shove the cork back in. An opened white wine put back in the fridge has a slightly higher life expectancy than a re-corked red, but the dismal rule still appears to be that nobody routinely tastes opened wine at the beginning of each service to check its condition. In the least scrupulous establishments, the hope presumably is that none of the punters will know whether the wine is supposed to taste like this anyway.

For far too long, there was no legal definition of what constituted a glass of wine. In a weights-and-measures culture that is micro-specific about the amount of head allowable on a pint of beer, and in which every bottle of standard spirit is mounted upside-down with a dispense-mechanism to measure out the exact 25ml (formerly one-sixth of a gill) a drinker is permitted in one go, the apportioning of wine by the glass was as slapdash as whisky-pouring always was in the rest of Europe. When the law was at last codified, two measures were provided for: the healthy 175ml (or just under a quarter of a bottle), and the unbearably parsimonious 125ml, the mingy little egg-cup the trade considers to be the lady's measure. Some places offer both; others – perhaps reluctant to splash out on two lots of glasses – stick with just one. Thus has confusion and unfairness been perpetuated. An establishment selling you 125ml as 'a glass of wine' without any other qualification is within the law. The (perfectly legal) catch is that they, and not you, have decided on what the measure shall be. You might have gritted your teeth and decided that £3.95 was just about acceptable for a glass of oaky Chilean Chardonnay: you may not realise you are about to be served an irritatingly mean measure.

With champagne, the path to abuse is still relatively obstacle-free. No standard measure exists here, and so it is possible (and highly likely) that when the celebration apéritif arrives you will be roundly disappointed to find you've been allotted a thimbleful. This may seem a little surprising, since one glass of fizz arguably leads to another one more easily than does one glass of dull table white. Then there is the thornier problem of how to keep it not just fresh but fizzy once the bottle has been opened. The champagne-saver bottle-cap is pretty efficient, but others may simply be relying on sticking a spoon in the top of the bottle – an old folk remedy from the era of treating bronchial chests by tying bundles of dried stinkweed around the neck, and about as efficacious – that is, not at all.

In any event, serving still or sparkling wine by the glass has been embraced so wholeheartedly these days because it offers pro-portionately an even greater profit margin than a whole bottle. The restaurateur or publican may rejoin that part of the mark-up covers the wastage in all those unfinished bottles, but the escalator is usually higher still. The actual economics might provoke indigestion in the unsuspecting drinker, but fortunately are not generally known. A bottle that may have cost about £2.50 wholesale is marked up to, say, £6 in a pub or £12 in a modest restaurant. Sold in 125ml glasses – of which there are six to a bottle – at £2 in the former and £4 in the latter, it is not hard to see how the insistence on wine by the glass, however much gets poured down the throats of the staff at the end of the evening, has played into the hands of the profiteers, especially if more than one glass is to be ordered. It may well be more economical for customers to order a whole bottle and leave what they don't want.

Drinking a glass of sparkling wine or dry white table wine as an appetite-sharpener is only a fairly recent phenomenon, though, in Britain. In generations past, our preferred pre-dinner wine tipple was a little glass of fortified wine. Possibly no apéritif in the world is more instantly, efficiently stimulating to the appetite than pale, bone-dry fino or manzanilla sherry. It is almost impossible not to eat something with it, even if only a handful of salty nuts. But if the service of table wines is often characterised by cack-handed ignorance, the service of dry sherry ought to be referred to the International Court of Justice. Not only is it always and invariably stale (the bottle having been open for a very long time because nobody ever orders it), but it is also hardly ever served chilled. Only about fifteen people in British catering have ever been taught that dry sherry is a dry white wine, and not a liqueur, and so it sits on the bar deteriorating over the months and years. Oxidation deepens its colour to an unnerving teak, while the nose is gradually transformed from freshly shelled peanuts to last Christmas's dry-roasted. In this parlous state, it has almost ceased to be a drink at all and become a kind of noxious chemical substance instead, serving only to add another pointless £3.50 to your bill. One way or another, then, the whole apéritif phase of eating out, which was to put an edge on the appetite, and create a relaxed, anticipatory mood, has now done exactly the opposite of what it was intended to.

Sooner or later, though, the preliminaries are over and done with, you've nibbled some bread and glanced at the menu. Now the waiter returns with a padded folder of considerably greater weight than the one you're already studying. Would you like to see the wine list?

Well, would you?

In some restaurants these days, particularly out in the sticks where a certain quirkiness often guarantees repeat business, it is possible to take your own wine. There are a few highly regarded hotel restaurants in the UK that have never quite seen the point of applying for a licence, and so if you wish to drink wine, you have no option but to BYOB, as if this were a 1970s dinner invitation. Others do have a wine cellar, but would rather you drink your own bottle of Jacob's Creek Chardonnay if that will stop you whinging about their prices. At one unlicensed Cumbrian establishment, the no-choice dinner menu kicks off at eight with a glass of sherry – complimentary, of course. But while encouraging diners to bring their own wine is a customer-friendly ploy, any goodwill will soon be dissipated as it emerges that the proprietor will almost certainly charge you for opening it. At least one London restaurant expects £8 a bottle.

If there is already a wine list, it's perhaps only fair to make a nominal charge for the serving of the wine and the use of their glasses, but corkage, as it is called, is another grey area. Should the table with its Jacob's Creek Chardonnay really be paying the same as the group bringing a carefully nursed bottle of fifteen-year-old claret that may well have thrown a sediment and require decanting? And if the restaurant doesn't have a licence, should it expect to make anything at all out of you drinking your own wine? In my opinion, a BYO wine policy is the sort of trick that looks good in the restaurant guides, but isn't particularly helpful in practice. It is always possible to ring ahead and ask what tonight's menu will be, but if there is a choice and you don't know what's going to be on offer, how will you know what to pick up at the off-licence? In any case, part of the joy of a good wine list is to discover wines that are not available in the high street, idiosyncratic bottles amassed by a conscientious and imaginative cellar master.

In fact, such lists are few and far between, and while the overall quality of restaurant wine lists is far higher than thirty or forty years ago – mirroring developments in the off-trade – the level of imagination has declined. In the UK there are now broadly four types of wine list:

(1) The Collector's Item;

(2) The Remainder Bin;

(3) The Global Grab-Bag;

(4) The Crown Jewels.

The first kind has already been referred to. Here, the restaurateur has sourced wines from any and every possible outlet. They will have come from wholesalers' lists, auction-rooms, private purchases, perhaps even buying trips to Europe, because this kind of list is compiled by someone with a genuinely insatiable passion for the subject, who would like his or her customers to share it. When such individuals' enthusiasm runs wild, the result can be wine lists lengthily annotated with their own Jilly Gooldenisms, heavily spattered with coloured stickers denoting wines that were only bought in twos or threes and have now run out, perhaps even flagged in far too many places with the provocative tag, 'POA' ('price on application'), meaning this wine has, since it was bought, quite possibly appreciated in value, as a result of which its list price is not stable. For all their infuriating unpredictability, these are often the great lists, the written evidence of an Aladdin's Cave cellar in which you will find just about anything you hanker after, if only you rummage long enough. Often, a bottle of some slightly dodgy old vintage can be made the subject of amiable negotiation, with the price dropped a little if the wine turns out not to be in quite perfect condition. I met one Lancashire restaurateur who took such an interest when his customers ordered certain wines that he insisted on sharing half a glass with them. Imagine the outraged indignation that would greet similar enthusiasm in a big metropolitan restaurant, where mine host would automatically be presumed to be simply a shameless chancer looking to get drunk at your expense.

The second category – the Remainder Bin – used to be the baleful rule in British restaurants until a generation ago, when the world began to change. These are the default lists on which you will find the kinds of wines I discussed in Chapter 3 – old famous names only too content to turn out oceans of mediocre dross for precisely this end of the market. Nowadays these wine lists have largely been driven back to the high-street trattorias and back-alley bistros of middling provincial towns – printed up back in around 1975, since which there has been no particular reason to change them, other than to inflate the prices now and then. Bought usually from one large wholesaler to whom wine is no more distinctive a commodity than malt vinegar or frozen prawns, the wines will span a quality range from the accidentally drinkable to the unutterably atrocious. At the former extreme will be the likes of Montepulciano d'Abruzzo or red Côtes du Rhône; at the latter, basic Muscadet and bulk Chianti take pride of place. The house wine will be some nameless filth from the south of France, a low-born vin de table scarcely worth troubling your liver to metabolise.

Almost inevitably, on these lists there will be no producers' names. Why would it matter who produced such insipid creations? In any case, the wholesaler may change suppliers every few years, and naming the producer would mean having the list expensively reprinted each time. For the same reason, there may well be no mention of vintages, as though the customer were invited to assume that all the whites were the youngest available and the reds suitably mature, whatever their age. More likely it is because the customer is presumed to be as ignorant as the proprietors about good and bad vintages. Admittedly, only a small minority of wine-literate patrons may keep such information in their heads at all times, but if all else fails, at least a stated vintage gives you the chance to judge how mature a wine might be. Having no such information makes the whole business a lottery, or requires the waiter to scurry back and forth to check a range of possible options before you take the plunge. These are not, by and large, establishments in which such punctiliousness will be appreciated. Indeed, as you dither between the '98 Montepulciano and the '99 Minervois, you may well detect an 'I-haven't-got-all-night-you-know' sigh, or even the 'God-we've-got-a-right-one-here' sigh. There is no earthly reason to allow places like this to make more than the minimum profit out of you on wine. Order the house wine, and hold your nose.

The third type of wine list, the Global Grab-Bag, is what most of the restaurants that crop up in the annual restaurant guides these days are running. Typically, it covers as little as one side of an A4 card, and is divided up no more pedantically than into reds and whites, with sparklers at the top and fortified wines at the bottom. Not for this sort of list the exigencies of geographical categorisation, multi-vintage runs of particular appellations or descriptive tasting notes. This is simply a happy jumble of bottles, usually arranged in ascending order of price, the implication being that you decide how much you want to spend, and then see what's available. There is tra-ditionally a roughly equal ratio of European (ie. French, Italian and Spanish) to New World (with California and Australia in the van-guard), but only a surprisingly restricted range of grape varieties. The varietal labelling of non-European wines is such that only the most internationally known grapes tend to come up, resulting in a red selection that is predominantly Cabernet Sauvignon, Merlot and Pinot Noir, with some Spanish and Italian interlopers nosing their way into the cracks, while the whites may be little more than Chardonnay and Sauvignon Blanc.

Some of these lists can be highly alluring, and the refusal to accord the classic regions of France any axiomatic pre-eminence over the rest of the world is definitely a progressive trend, but certain wines – or types of wines – do tend to feature with monotonous reliability. The list will be ankle-deep in oaked Chardonnay, together with heavily oaked reds from the hot countries. Lighter wines such as Côte de Beaune burgundies, *cru* Beaujolais, Loire reds, Italian Dolcetto or Barbera, the more 'neutral' varietals of Alsace such as Pinot Blanc or Sylvaner, or German Riesling are generally conspicuous by their absence, sunk without trace in the deluge of Shiraz, Zinfandel and barrel-fermented Chardonnay, all seeking to outdo each other with their 13.5-14% alcohol quotients. This is a great shame, since the aforementioned wines are often distinctly better suited to food than the knuckle-trailers, but here big, brash wines are as much the mood of the moment as in any international wine competition. (Among those lighter wines, sightings of German Riesling – once a constituent part of any serious wine list – are now rarer than the black rhinoceros. Nobody lists good German wines any longer, partly because of the widespread derision for Liebfraumilch and its ilk, and perhaps also because they are falsely seen as unsuitable for pairing with food. And yet most possess greater longevity, and a sight more complexity, than the oaky Chardonnays.)

The fourth and final type of wine list, the Crown Jewels, is the paradigm most of us have in mind when dreaming of what will be on offer at the three-Michelin-starred or 10-point *Good Food Guide* restaurant. In this hallowed inventory Zinfandel and Shiraz are foreign coinages – indeed, so are any names of grape varieties. Instead, the commodities it trades in are châteaux and domaines, with the same names often being glorified in flights of successive vintages. France is respectfully anatomised into its component regions, with 'les vins de Bourgogne' and 'les vins du Bordelais' heading the roll of honour. The prices will reflect not only the pedigree of the wines, but also quite possibly the London postcode where you are eating, and the four-figure barrier will be breached with scarcely a blush. If other countries are permitted a walk-on part, they will take their place as the bit-part players they are, providing price relief perhaps for the under-resourced, but parading in their lonely ones and twos under the faintly gauche headings of 'La Nouvelle Zélande' and 'L'Afrique du Sud', like tiny island nations at an Olympic marchpast.

At the zenith of the Crown Jewels lists are mature vintages of classed-growth Bordeaux and *grand cru* burgundies, at prices that thrill with their shameless obscenity. What sommelier would ever believe you could afford the bottle of 1970 Château Mouton-Rothschild or the half of 1959 Château d'Yquem, were you to order one up? Imagine sending it back on the grounds that it was out of condition, *a little over-oxidised*, perhaps, or developing *a fugitive hint of mustiness* . . . In fact, the rule with such ancient bottles tends to be *Caveat emptor* (Let the buyer beware), much as it is at auction. So the 30-year-old claret smells like a dishcloth and tastes of old mushrooms? Tough. It might have been wiser to stick to the Chilean Cabernet.

Whether to risk £2,000 on a bottle of old claret is a dilemma the great majority of us will never have to face. That doesn't mean that wine prices in restaurants are not a cause for concern. Indeed, virtually no aspect of eating out arouses more indignation, more affront and more sighing, weary cynicism. It isn't hard to understand why. The mark-up on the wholesale price at which most restaurant wine is charged is enjoyed by scarcely any other retail item. In London, it is commonly 250-350% of the price in the shop – and bear in mind that the proprietor is not paying the retail price. A bottle of industrial-grade Soave that probably cost him something like £2, and can be bought in the off-licence for around £4, may well appear on his list in the £12-15 bracket. The more you go for quality, however – so the theory runs – the better the value, since a three-and-a-half-times mark-up on a £60 bottle of champagne would put it at £210, but a restaurant may settle for relieving you of a mere £125. This is supposed to encourage us to trade up. However, the concomitant side of the equation is less edifying to dwell on. From him that hath not, it would seem, shall be taken even that which he hath. If you can only afford Soave – or, more demeaning still, house wine – you obviously deserve to be skinned.

But why?

The standard defence the restaurant trade has offered over the years is that wine mark-ups are the only area in which they are properly able to make the profit that enables them to survive. Not merely the food and drink and the wages of the staff must be budgeted for. There are fuel and lighting, laundry, business rates, periodic re-decorations and insurance to take into account, as well as all the other small items like candles, matchbooks, lavatory essentials and stationery. Were all these factors to be considered when it came to menu pricing, nobody in Britain would eat out ever again. Many smaller restaurants, it is argued, grudgingly make a loss on much of the food they serve, when all the elements in its preparation and serving are set against the prices charged for it. Even if a modest profit can be made from the food, the crucial margin determining the difference between a comfortable living and mere survival from year to year must be derived from what are airily referred to as the 'incidentals'. These include bottled water, bar drinks, coffee, perhaps cigars – and inevitably wine. In addition to service, a cover charge may be loaded on, justified implicitly by the bread-basket that comes round as often as it is bidden, the dish of olives you have made short work of, and even perhaps the little unexpected appetisers (or *amuse-bouches*, as a more effete era knew them) that arrive before any of the ordered food. These days, these little extras are increasingly being cut out, as are the battalions of petits fours that once heralded the arrival of coffee, so that what you order is what you get, *tout court*.

The cover charge, itself subject to service once the final bill is tallied, may at last be dying out, but in many places has been replaced by charges for bread. If you want another bit of ciabatta, you must pay again. Separate charges for vegetables, once seemingly beaten back to the most unreconstructed Italian trattorias, where the implication was that if you really needed a plate of sautéed potatoes or deep-fried zucchini to go with your microwaved dish of bubbling cheese you jolly well ought to pay for it, are staging a recovery. City brasseries now routinely charge £4 for a tiny dish of mashed potato or buttered spinach, and perhaps £4 more for a bowl of salad leaves, inflating the price of the main course by maybe two-thirds. All of this should have an implication for wine pricing. It reflects, after all, a growing realisation that the market won't bear price inflation falling exclusively on wine indefinitely. Wines by the glass, discussed earlier, have been another solution, and yet, far more than £2 for a bread roll or £5 for a bottle of Evian, wine still represents a restaurateur's best chance of making serious money out of his customers.

One of the principal reasons is that the true price of any given wine is still, to most patrons, very much a mystery wrapped in an enigma. Having bought a bottle in Oddbins for £7.50, we can drink it and decide for ourselves if it was worth the outlay, and therefore whether we would buy it again. Adjusting ourselves to the economics of the wine list, we splash out £20 on a bottle, similarly hoping that it will be a rewardingly complex and food-friendly specimen. The difference is that you don't know what the retail value of this restaurant wine is, and so you may very well be ordering a less exalted wine than you think you are. Were you to learn it had cost the proprietor a fiver, you might find an attack of dyspepsia coming on. It is therefore very much in a restaurateur's best interests to stock wines that are not usually found in the high street. This is why it's better not to list too many of the dreary old European names. It doesn't matter who made the Chianti or the Muscadet, nor indeed what the vintages are: most diners have a clear and fixed idea of what Chianti and Muscadet should cost. On the other hand, wines from the less well-known corners of Europe – Spain's Somontano, for example, Italy's Puglia or the Alentejo of southern Portugal, not to mention virtually the entire panoply of southern-hemisphere wines from the new producers – are a boon to the restaurateur, given their crucial combination of low unit cost and commercial invisibility.

Various ruses have been tried by restaurants aware of how much indignation is aroused by mark-ups on wine. A dipstick policy has been tried here and there, which involved charging pro rata for the amount of wine drunk from a bottle that wasn't finished. It hasn't caught on, largely because it doesn't represent a real saving. The percentage mark-up is still the same, even if you only swallow a mouthful, and in any case, at least one establishment applied a flat-rate surcharge on top of the pro-rata price to cover the inevitable wastage. And, left to one's own devices, with a suitably long wait before pudding and only one of you driving, who wouldn't finish the bottle in front of them? The outcome might well be, therefore, that that two-thirds of a bottle of superior wine you had intended to pay for becomes a whole bottle you can't afford. Half-bottles are another ruse, on which a more handsome profit can be made, and yet, dessert wines aside, most restaurant lists are still curiously deficient in them. Some wine industries, notably in Italy but also many of the newer producers, are reluctant to bottle wine in halves, but nonetheless there is enough wine about in smaller capacities to offer a genuine choice. And yet lists are often restricted to two or three in each colour. Wine by the glass has emerged as the natural solution, for the simple reason that, as we have seen, the tills are made to ring more exultantly.

Martin Lam, chef-proprietor of Ransome's Dock restaurant in south London, is one who believes that restaurateurs could quite easily offer customers a better deal on wine. He runs a wine list that not only constitutes demonstrably good value, especially in the capital, but also is one that is widely commended by the restaurant guides for its depth and range. To what did he attribute his accolades? 'I just buy better wines that might cost more,' he replies, 'but are marked up less.' The ten-page list is prefaced with a slate of 'Ransome's Dock Selections', wines that, as at August 2000, ranged from £13.50 to £20. These are not intended as house wines, but rather have been picked out to represent what the list is trying to do. Lam insists that he makes a maximum 60% gross profit on these wines, never more, a margin that comes down dramatically on certain of the ritzier offerings. 'It works like a dream, partly because people don't feel they're getting second-best. They're not just having house wine.' Because the price/quality ratio of these wines is so attractive, they sell in correspondingly healthy quantities. It is a simple enough equation: extract a smaller margin from any commodity, and you will augment the market for it, leading – with any luck – to a greater overall return. The point, though, is that all the wines on his list have been selected for class. You are not being invited to up the ante for a French classic simply in order to escape the clutches of Côtes de Gascogne or Frascati.

Lam's establishment is as subject to the vagaries of restaurant economics as any other place is. 'If we were to sell no wine at all,' he confesses, 'it would be hard to survive, but we aim to achieve a comfortable mix of margins on food and wine, instead of piling it all on to the wine.' There is no naïve sense of charity about what Lam is doing. What he has recognised, however, is an image problem that astonishingly few places seem motivated to address. 'The perception is that restaurants are greedy, that they are making a killing on wine. But if it matters to us to be seen to be offering value in what we do, then value for money should be perceptible at all levels.' For the time being, the likes of Martin Lam can bask in the honour that comes from going against the grain. What he is doing is nothing more revolutionary than undercutting his competitors, but it remains something of an indictment of the restaurant sector that such an initiative seems incapable of provoking a trend. There are, after all, only so many people who can pack his restaurant each evening. The rest must go to be ripped off elsewhere. It would only take one of the upmarket chains – that is, the very operators who could most afford to follow Lam's example – to start charging appreciably less for wine, and a full-scale price war might break out. Somehow, though, this remains as unlikely as expecting a fair deal from the rail companies. If the market will seemingly tolerate extortion, why rock the boat?

If it were only the price that raised hackles when it came to drinking wine in restaurants. Other aspects of wine service, however, have been annoying people for generations, and yet are still practised today as though a *sine qua non* of successful catering. Most irritating of all is undoubtedly topping up. Some have wondered whether the practice is not an over-zealous impulse to courtesy, on a par with having the napkin spread across your lap as you sit down. Topping up a glass when no more than two or three sips have been taken out of it is nothing whatsoever to do with courtesy. It is about urging you to drink up and finish this bottle, so that – finding yourself dry in the middle of the main course – you might be coerced into ordering more. In the sense that any table ordering a single bottle of wine and no more will have intended it to match the main courses, the wine is largely being traduced. It arrives way in advance of any food, and thus mostly accompanies the bread. If a second bottle is ordered, the greater part of it will still be left after the main courses are done, and it will now be drunk before and after desserts, or more likely abandoned altogether. The only solution is to tell the waiter that you would like the wine to be served with the appropriate course. If you are ignored, at least you will know that this is not an establishment that takes wine seriously. Forcing claret down you while you are embarked on a light crab soufflé is as stupid as putting it in an ice bucket.

Which receptacle, meanwhile, is another bone of contention. Some places insist on putting all white wines in a bucket, which may well result in over-chilling by the time the wine is scarcely half-drunk. It may be nice for sparkling wines and for the very sweetest dessert wines, but can easily vacuum the subtleties out of a delicate dry white. Ice buckets are there to look good, to justify the silly money you are being asked to part with for the wine by the opulence of its conveyance. The ice bucket also makes serving yourself with your own wine trickier, and if there is one thing almost as annoying as over-eager replenishment, it is gormless negligence when the bottle is not readily accessible. At some grand establishments, the bottle – with or without bucket – may be removed to a central serving-area, to be retrieved every time a fill-up looks necessary. In these circumstances, to be made to sit with an empty glass while you frustratedly try to get the waiter to notice is unforgivable.

It is not the done thing in the Gavroche to pour your own wine. But in 1992, a colleague and I sat there with empty glasses, staring at our bottle of Chablis, which had been set up at the far edge of our enormous round table. We couldn't quite reach it without committing the equally scandalous faux pas of rising slightly in our seats.

The aching, empty minutes ticked on, we raised our drained glasses to our lips in suppliant appeal, but to no avail. Finally, we cracked. At the risk of causing apoplexy all around us, I half-stood and reached across the table. As if by magic, the absconded sommelier reappeared to snatch the bottle from my hand with an imperious 'Please', and the glasses were at last refilled. The thin, crappy Chablis we had paid over £30 for now went down like the vinegar of contrition. I was a living reincarnation of some long-forgotten Bateman cartoon: *The Man Who Tried To Pour His Own Wine in Le Gavroche*.

However small one may be made to feel by incidents like these, they are as nothing to the way restaurants have historically treated women when it comes to wine. Certainly, in the homes where it was drunk, wine was traditionally a male preserve, but this has not been exclusively the case for at least a generation now. Nevertheless, in restaurants up and down the land, on every night of the week, it is the male half of a mixed couple who will be handed the wine list and given the wine to taste on opening, even if the woman has ordered it. This is indeed a peculiar custom, not least because in this country women drank wine on evenings out long before men could be tempted away from their pints without fearing accusations of homosexuality. Two women eating together may well find themselves denied the courtesy of checking the condition of the wine, or treated with a certain patient scepticism if they venture to suggest it might be faulty. Old-school Italian restaurants were the very worst offenders in this regard, and often seemed to believe that women – or British women, specifically – had no capacity for wine. A woman dining alone is still widely presumed to have been stood up or let down in some way by a man. If she appears to be drowning her sorrows by calling for a bottle of Brunello di Montalcino, her tragedy is thereby confirmed. Still, if she is lucky, she may have her spirits buoyed all evening by the mosquito-like persistence of a waiter with an enormous pepper-grinder.

None of the foregoing is to deny that the provision of wine in restaurants is vastly improved from the days when the wine books set out to try to save you from the arrogance of unsympathetic sommeliers. But until restaurateurs give us the impression that they actually want us to enjoy drinking wine with their food, rather than using it to extract a rapacious return, there will be always be lingering resentment. The point must continue to be made, by consumer groups, the annual restaurant guides and by customers themselves: WINE IN RESTAURANTS COSTS TOO MUCH. Depending on where we are eating, the cost may be anything from mildly excessive to grand larceny, but the restaurants where it is possible to drink wine for a price that seems fair to proprietor and customer alike, are shamingly few. Until the matter is treated with less cynicism, it will stand as a rebuke to the whole industry.

Chapter 8

MARRIAGE GUIDANCE

Or: How food and wine matching
turned into an exact science

MY PARENTS HARDLY EVER DRANK wine at home. They hardly ever drank anything at home, tending to see the consumption of alcohol as something for social activities like eating out or family get-togethers. Occasionally, my father would surprise and delight us by buying a bottle of something to drink with Sunday lunch. I can remember distinctly a sinking sensation on the Sundays when the bottle turned out to be sparkling apple juice instead. The one occasion, however, on which there would reliably be wine was Christmas Day, when caution was thrown to the winds and we drank before, during and after lunch. And what we drank with the roast turkey, year after year, was Asti Spumante.

There was no gastronomic consideration at work. We had Asti

because it was a fizzy wine, got up in a bottle with a wire cage over the cork, and it therefore looked the part. It was a wine of celebration on account of its bubbles, but I'm not sure if any of us took in the fact that it was sweet, let alone whether it actually 'went' with the turkey. What was important was the feeling of living it up. Even at its famously low alcohol level, when drunk in the middle of the day the wine had its effect, as my mother invariably discovered when she subsided semi-recumbent on to the settee with the plaintive announcement, 'My head's *whizzing*.' These formative years left me with a lifelong taste for Asti, so much so that I won't hear a word said against it, and we still have it with Christmas dinner, although it now goes with the pudding.

Indeed, there simply isn't a better match with the traditional Christmas pudding than sparkling Asti. As I tell people whenever I can, it works because the fizz helps to slice through the suety density of the pudding, the sweetness factor is exactly right where rotted dessert wines such as Sauternes go merely sickly in its presence, and after the preceding onslaught of champagne and red and white wines, the low alcohol is just what's needed. However, this is virtually the only example of a food and wine match about which I am prepared to be so assured. Otherwise, the range of possible combinations is legion, but increasingly – as the whole issue has been subjected to relentless pseudo-scientific research – that reassuring diversity of partnerships has been taken from us. What was once the happy and convivial business of matchmaking in the matter of food and wine has now become marriage guidance, as an earnest soul-searching has taken over. More time is wasted, more navelgazing piffle spouted, over this question than in any other aspect of wine commentary. It has become, quite literally in some contexts, a whole industry in itself. When the British began drinking wine again in the 1960s, the only rule of thumb you needed to know was, 'red wine with meat, white with fish'. As a student, I remember hearing the first subtle modulation of this rubric from the mouths of London chums who might have been presumed to know. This was, 'red wine with red meats, white with white meats and fish'. That sounded a logical enough elaboration of the basic rule, although not one that could be readily tried on visits home, since, for the first 65 years of his life, my father wouldn't go near red wine. Soon afterwards, though, in the democratic backlash against any sort of specialism that is still very much one of the idiosyncrasies of the British character, one heard it said that the whole business was a lot of mystificatory hoodoo, and that the important thing was to drink whatever you enjoyed, regardless of whether it seemed to be a suitable gustatory match. And why not? This is after all what wine, far more than any other alcoholic drink, has been about at least since biblical times. That laissez-faire approach, I am quite sure, is still very much the order of the day in most homes, but it is not any more the official line. These days, the question of what to drink with what has expanded to fill a large part of the syllabus, and the school term shows no sign of coming to an end.

An introductory guide to wine is now expected to have a whole section on food and wine matching (as indeed does mine). The food and cookery magazines now feel obligated to run a small box or paragraph under each recipe or dinner-party menu suggesting wines that would go well with the featured dishes. These have become so widespread, even in magazines whose readers would not be thought the natural constituency for wine recommendations, that there is, as I can readily vouch, a modest monthly stipend to be made from writing them. In the specialist wine magazines, whole features are given over to convocations of beetle-browed experts munching and sipping in selfless deliberation. Of these, more later. Now, whole books are being published on the subject. At first it was tentative little paperbacks under the supermarkets' own imprints; now there are lavishly designed coffee-table hardbacks that leave no stone unturned in their exhaustiveness.

But the only question that needs to be addressed on this matter of food with wine is how deeply into it you wish to go. It is undeniably true that considering a particular match in minute sensory detail offers conclusions to be drawn. Comparative evaluation of just two examples of almost any commodity, be it wines or sexual positions, will establish that one seems to be preferable to the other. The agony only begins when you try to pinpoint exactly why this should be so. With food and wine matching, a whole host of complicated factors comes into play, which necessarily requires a fine-tuned understanding of the dynamics of taste for any elucidation. I am not sure that even most wine writers eat and drink in this way when they sit down to dinner, but I am perfectly sure humanity in general has no desire to do so. To the pontificating journalist solemnly advising us, 'The acid edge on the Vouvray sec did not make a happy bedfellow with the coruscating pungency of the coriander dressing, but we were gratified to note that the Spätlese Riesling, for which both Jocasta and myself had predicted a bitter fate, came to no harm at all, its residual sweetness positively romping through the herbaceousness,' we may safely sneer, 'Get a life'. And that means you too, Jocasta.

It all goes back to the blurb on the label. When the supermarkets changed the world by adding back-labels to bottles of European wine advising you roughly (very roughly) what it would taste like, what it was made from and how long you might prudently keep it, there was usually a pay-off line suggesting what you might like to drink it with. Nowadays, this advice is still no more precise than it was when it started appearing. The French, particularly, for all their vaunted nicety in gastronomic judgement, often turn out to be surprisingly broad-brush in their suggestions. 'Drink with casseroles, red meat dishes and cheeses,' suggests the English-language label on the back of a bottle of Corbières, although in Britain casserole cookery hasn't been fashionable for the last ten years, and cheeses might mean anything from a chalky little goat number to a scatological soft Burgundian thing oozing its way around the board. Other labels, in trying to stimulate the imagination with much more specific guidance, end up sounding a little too clever: 'a good match for sushi and shellfish and ideal with all types of fish in creamy sauces, Chicken Véronique or Chicken Caesar salad.' That too was on a French bottle, but one wearing a very New World livery, and labelled Bordeaux Sauvignon, rather than Château Quelquechose. *Chicken Véronique*, please note, rather than sole, and Caesar salad with chicken rather than just croutons, Parmesan and perhaps the odd gobbet of anchovy, are what this wine was destined for. The obvious problem with being too specific is that the wine may be hastily put back on the shelf if you don't feel like chicken tonight, and had already bought a pair of salmon fishcakes. Instead, the middle way is to combine an apparent specificity with a panoramic sweep across several food categories, so that nobody need feel left out. 'Ideal with fish, seafood, grilled chicken, other white meats and sautéed vegetables,' claims a Chilean Chardonnay, while a Portuguese red assures the dithering buyer that it 'will accompany almost any fuller-flavoured dishes, for example, roasts, barbecue, cheese, pasta and vegetarian'. 'Roast what?' we may wonder. 'Barbecued what?' It doesn't seem to matter. This is a shameless hussy of a wine, happy to go with 'almost any' type of food, no matter what the sauce on that pasta, no matter what the vegetarian delicacy. The indifference as to what vegetarians might be advised to drink shows a little insultingly in that reduction of an entire eating regimen to one generic food type. When it comes to serving suggestions, these labels might as well just say, 'Whatever', and have done with it.

The truth is that, just as there is no such thing as an invariably successful recipe, only one that turns out a little differently every time you cook it, neither is there any foolproof match of food and wine. This is at least partly because, as the French proverb has it, there are no good wines, only good bottles of wine. No two bottles of the same grower's Châteauneuf-du-Pape from the same vintage taste exactly alike, let alone the Châteauneuf-du-Papes from different growers, and still less those from different vintages. What works once may not succeed the next time, and the elements in a recipe that most affect the balance of overall flavours – namely the various seasonings – vary widely from one occasion to the next. You might buy the best free-range corn-fed chicken every time, but do you really measure out the quantity of tarragon in the stuffing, or regulate its freshness to the day? And did the wine have an hour in an open decanter, or was its cork drawn immediately before the chicken was served? Such manifold variability gives the lie to the idea that food and wine matching can ever resemble a science, to be conducted with empirical precision. The food and wine writers may confess that there are ultimately no rules – but if there aren't, then how can any sound conclusions be drawn, and what is the point of devoting whole articles and books to it?

At the large-scale Fetzer winery in Mendocino County, California, there is a wine-school that includes in its prospectus classes in food and wine matching. Under-occupied West Coasters sign up in droves, and are encouraged to taste and evaluate without preconceptions, chewing and slurping in agonised earnest, in order to establish whether unoaked Sauvignon is a more apposite foil than lightly oaked Viognier for the 'erbs in a goats' cheese and cilantro quiche. How did we ever arrive at this cringe-making, masturbatory display?

The answer, in Europe at least, is something to do with heritage and a due sense of breeding. Even more than the self-appointed Brahmins of Mendocino County, the late Count Matuschka-Greiffenclau of the Schloss Vollrads winery in Germany's Rheingau was fiercely punctilious on such matters. In the historic estate's restaurant, the Graues Haus, he once bored me rigid over dinner insisting I tried one different cuvée after another with each of the myriad courses, brooking absolutely no dissent. I didn't think the dry Riesling was that great a match for the nettle bavarois with smoked eel, and made the grave mistake of saying so. In *Reflections on the Harmony of Food and Wine*, a booklet summarising Matuschka's collected wisdom in matters gastronomic, we learn, familiarly enough, that there are no immutable rules. 'A light red wine can be paired with baked fish, just as a dry Riesling Spätlese is an excellent partner for leg of lamb in a sauce seasoned with rosemary.' The first suggestion may be fairly conceded, though the latter seems to me more the crossed-fingered hope of the spokesman for a wine culture notably poor in suitable red wines. Soon, though, the booklet's pronouncements take on the tone of holy writ, and it seems that immutable rules are there to be obeyed after all. 'Anyone who enjoys goose liver with a Sauternes or a rich Auslese should steam the liver and serve it with apple rings and a honey sauce after the main course.' I further tried the Count's patience by saying that I didn't feel such considerations really mattered in the grand scheme of things, and only served to make wine appreciation less enjoyable. This produced a spasm of despair: a whole generation was coming to maturity that knew nothing of these issues, just as nobody was prepared to sit around a table *en famille* any more to eat. As it turned out, I was the last British journalist to interview Matuschka. About three weeks later, he went to a lonely place in the vineyard and shot himself.

Of course certain wines go obligingly with certain dishes. But it is more the case that very few combinations actually clash. Matching the degree of acidity in a wine with the degree of acidity in a dressing, especially anything involving tomato, can be tricky, and then there is a broader textural consideration to be aware of. Some wines are just too light or, conversely, too rich to make an adequate match with a dish. Sometimes the forthright flavour of some principal ingredient, or more usually some seasoning, upsets the flavour of a wine, leaving it with an underminingly bitter, or harshly metallic, aftertaste. These are the reactions to be aware of, the Don'ts rather than the Dos, and there is more consistency here than there ever can be in deciding in what makes a positive juxtaposition. Every single time I have attended an official food and wine tasting, it has turned up at least one complete surprise, often involving wines that one would have thought too delicate in the circumstances. Champagne and soup is a combination not much advised in the manuals, and yet I have found a blanc de noirs champagne acquiring extra richness and depth when drunk alongside a richly creamy 'cappuccino' of wild mushrooms. Even more bemusingly, a subtly flavoured rosé opened out beautifully on the palate alongside a bowl of earthy leek and potato soup. A mature *cru* Beaujolais from Morgon once created a world of savoury satisfaction when drunk with plainly roasted beef and a horseradish dressing, even though no guide you will ever look at will allow that Beaujolais has the weight to cope with beef. Tried again on another occasion, the combinations might well fail, but what arrests the attention is the fact that, in each case, the match became greater than the sum of its parts. This is the Holy Grail of such exercises, and one not often encountered.

When the specialist journals stage such tastings, however, they only rarely concern themselves with matters as prosaic as simple roast beef. In the early 1990s, a culture change, led by *WINE* magazine, overcame the whole enterprise. Suddenly, the focus was less on handing down solid advice on which kinds of wines to drink with staple foods, and more on commissioning a celebrity chef to produce a range of original dishes linked by some tenuous theme, with the recipes included in the feature. When the new Australian cuisine arrived in London and enjoyed its momentary burst of fame, *WINE* ran a tasting to discover the best wines to drink with recipes for kangaroo fillet and crocodile. In a trend-setting Hampstead restaurant at the same time, I took part in a strawberry session, at which the bill of fare included swordfish sautéed with strawberries, duck livers with strawberries marinated in balsamic vinegar, and strawberry-garnished goats' cheese, finishing with a white chocolate and strawberry gâteau. We mixed and matched the combinations from a table forested with bottles and, at the end of it, all strawberried out, I went home and was vilely sick. On another occasion, Anton Mosimann was invited to create an off-the-wall Christmas dinner menu, and we sat and deliberated over it in a private room at his Belgravia club. In classic fashion, Mosimann had produced a deconstructed, minimalist menu that centred on a course consisting of a single slice of turkey garnished with bits of green spring onion. We sipped and deliberated over the opulent wines, and set to wondering how many of the magazine's readers would be tempted to try these recipes on their unsuspecting families this Christmas, and how many of those three would furthermore order the sumptuous Puligny-Montrachet *premier cru*, La Tartouillade, from Isle of Muck Wines at £36.95 a bottle, which the majority of us had felt was the perfect match for Mosimann's tiny mouthfuls.

There might be some point in all this if the tastings at least tried to cut down wine and food matching myths, or set out to find wines that go with foods seen as notorious enemies of wine, but on the rare occasions they do, the waters are muddied by over-elaboration. For its April 2000 issue, *Decanter* set out to see whether wines could be found to go with egg dishes – a worthy enough enterprise for those who can't get through breakfast without a glass of something, or for whom the title of Elizabeth David's late work,

An Omelette and a Glass of Wine, struck a chord. But instead of going in search of savoury omelettes or scrambled eggs with smoked salmon, perhaps, we were summoned to the top-floor restaurant at Harvey Nichols and regaled with smoked quail's eggs, sea-urchin soufflé, chargrilled baby leeks with romesco sauce and soft-boiled egg, and steak tartare (the last containing, least detectably, a raw egg yolk, as well as Tabasco, cayenne pepper, capers and shallots and, for our souped-up Harvey Nic's version, an extravagant outer coat of sliced black truffle). The quails' eggs were best with a Spätlese Riesling from the Mosel, but the soufflé was harder to please, with only a blanc de blancs champagne coming anywhere near fitting the bill, although I see from the write-up that 'Walton felt it tasted "oddly sweet"'. Walton also wondered who in their right minds cared.

The *Decanter* tasting was a bright idea, nevertheless, at least in the sense that eggs have traditionally been thought to present problems for wine. To be sure, it would be hard to imagine why anybody should want to drink a glass of wine with a boiled egg, whatever the time of day, but there are dishes with which it does seem appropriate. For a period during the 1990s, it was the height of food fashion to serve all sorts of dishes, particularly first courses, with a soft-poached egg as garnish. That could easily play havoc with a delicate white wine, and wasn't particularly nice with a richly oaky one. An oaked Chardonnay or similar was better with the butteriness of classically made scrambled eggs, especially if they contained strips of smoked salmon. What didn't especially work in that context was what many consider the dish's traditional partner, champagne. Both the egg and the smoked salmon denuded a delicate champagne of its subtleties, leaving it a vapid, acid shadow of its true self. It would be hard to imagine a worse waste of money.

A food and wine match can only really go wrong for two reasons: either because something in the food reacts badly with something in the wine, producing an unpleasant conflict on the palate, or because one of the two components easily overwhelms the other. Most people are fairly adept at imagining that particular wines will out-shout particular dishes, but may find it harder to see that the aggression can flow in the other direction. It doesn't take much ingenuity to see that a 14.5% Australian Shiraz will not be the most sympathetic match for a steamed fillet of white fish, but it is less evident that smoked salmon is too strong for a light, crisp champagne. Smoked salmon is not a delicately flavoured or textured food. It is oily, salty and smoky, and works correspondingly better with robustly constituted wines such as barrel-fermented Chardonnay or Gewurztraminer from Alsace. That said, it is never included on the roll-call of foods that fight with wine.

Under the old common consensus, the trickiest items to find partners for, apart from eggs, were held to be salads with vinaigrette dressings, anything in an emulsified sauce such as hollandaise or béarnaise, artichoke, chocolate, fresh fruit salads, and frozen desserts such as ice-creams, sorbets and parfaits. The fashion now, however, in guides to the subject, is to refuse to admit defeat, and insist that there are perfectly good partners for any of them, which may make one wonder how the rumours about incompatibility with wine ever got about in the first place.

Vinaigrettes were held to be a problem because the acidulating element in the oil – be it vinegar or lemon juice – created a painfully obvious clash with the wine's own acidity. A red or white wine vinegar was better than any other sort, such as cider vinegar, at least until the advent in British kitchens of the now ubiquitous balsamic (which has a sweeter, oaky flavour), while the fruitiness of lemon juice was thought to be friendlier still. Best of all, advised a few commentators, was to use whatever wine you were going to drink as the acid element in the dressing. This wasn't a bad suggestion with certain white wines such as crisp, leafy Sauvignon, but wasn't very convincing with sturdy reds, whose tannic astringency tasted very odd on lettuce leaves. One much-consulted guide affirms baldly that vinegar in a dressing 'destroys' the flavour of wine, which sits somewhat uneasily with the advice in a Sainsbury's pocket wine guide that there are 'first-class' matches to be made with such wines as Chablis and Sancerre, and 'quite good' matches with, amongst others, *premier cru* Chablis, New Zealand Sauvignon and Alsace Riesling. Even champagne is held to be 'adequate'. None of these is a wine cheap enough to risk its destruction in a failed marriage with a vinaigrette, and yet the sheer range of painstakingly researched choices suggests the picture is at least a little more nuanced than the old-school prophecy of doom would have it. My own view is that a subtle vinaigrette on a first-course salad built around a variety of boldly flavoured ingredients is not a problem for an assertively flavoured unoaked white wine, such as Sauvignon Blanc, Riesling or Chenin Blanc, particularly from the southern-hemisphere countries. Fighting fire with fire in terms of acidity seems, improbably, to result in better combinations than serving an apologetic little wine like Soave with an acidic dressing. A simple salad of leaves served as an intermediate course, and dressed with a vinaigrette that includes mustard and even garlic, emphatically doesn't need an accompanying wine.

With emulsified sauces, we are back in the realms of egg, and the problems that its yolky richness are held to create for wines. In fact, most of the hollandaise-type sauces are much more about butter than egg, with béarnaise in particular dominated by the flavour of fresh tarragon. One guide suggests that older wines will come to grief in the company of béarnaise, but doesn't appear to baulk at the idea of wine with hollandaise, even served with the dreaded artichoke. The Sainsbury writers report a dulling of aroma and neutralising of flavour in the case of many white wines, and declare red wines a complete no-no. The *Decanter* egg-and-wine panel I sat on also tested the fashionable brunch dish, eggs Benedict (a poached egg with ham on a muffin draped with hollandaise sauce), with a range of wines, and turned up one outstanding – and inevitably totally unpredictable – match. While the Sainsbury guide advises simple, unoaked white burgundy or similar Chardonnay from elsewhere, we discovered at Harvey Nic's that Jean-Philippe Fichet's Meursault Les Gruyaches 1997, with its layers of buttery, oaky opulence, was exactly the right match. On a restaurant wine list, it may well cost you in the region of eight times the dish itself, but at least you will be able to order with confidence.

Globe artichoke does have a very strange effect on wine. The outer leaves, plucked off and dipped in nothing more than a little lemony melted butter, don't present difficulties, but the heart does. Its bitter, even metallic taste has the peculiar effect of making almost any wine taste sweeter than it really is. Pickled baby artichokes in a salad seem even more of a threat to wine. Basic red or rosé is quite sufficient, suggests one guide, which even allows for a simple young claret if the artichoke is served with a traditional vinaigrette. This is an unspeakably dreadful combination, the bitterness of the artichoke, the acid edge of the vinegar and the stalky, raw tannin of basic Bordeaux adding up to a smorgasbord of horror on the palate. Another guide avoids red altogether. A southern French rosé might work, but the optimum combination is with an Australian dry Riesling, where presumably the sweetening effect of the aftertaste can be compensated by the naturally high acidity in the wine.

A dessert made with good chocolate, such as a mousse, tart, marquise or bavarois, was often thought to overwhelm all the subtleties in great sweet wine. Some consensus has now emerged for Orange Muscats from Australia or California as acceptable pairings. Australian Liqueur Muscats can also be good. In their sticky, marmaladey way, they constitute an equally powerful, but complementary partner. One guide suggests Bual madeira, which doesn't work half as well. There is a cheesy pungency about the sweetest styles of madeira that simply tastes rather stale and dank in the presence of chocolate. To be avoided at all costs with chocolate is anything red. The Sainsbury's writers suggest LBV port with chocolate mousse or bavarois. To most palates, this will seem a rebarbative clash, the tannin, peppery rasp and hot alcohol of red port taking all the lush indulgence off the chocolate flavour. The fortified sweet reds of southern France, Banyuls and Maury, promoted recently as fine companions to chocolate, are useless for much the same reasons. Violet-scented Black Muscat from California, another much-touted suggestion a few years ago, essentially failed because it was too thin in texture. What nobody suggests is Sauternes, the greatest dessert wine of them all, which for my money works beautifully with a dense, truffly mixture of high-octane cocoa solids. It has the weight and alcohol to cope with the power of chocolate, and enough acidity to prevent the resulting combination from seeming too cloying.

It is the natural acidity in fresh fruits, like that of tomatoes, that makes them a hazard to wine. Here, I wonder why you would want to obscure the pleasure to be had from ripe seasonal fruits by complicating them with another flavour. Even a fruit salad in a light, scented syrup doesn't need the adjunct of wine. Some commentators have even suggested wines for drinking with a single fruit eaten in the hand, such as a peach or nectarine. (One wonders whether such authorities are able to put anything in their mouths without an accompanying glass of wine. Is there a wine to go with an extra-strong mint on a train journey? And what does one drink with toothpaste?) Botrytised Rieslings or Asti are called into play by one guide, while another plumps for Chenin or Muscat. Red wine with raspberries was trendy a few years ago and, as long as you don't sugar and cream them, does work improbably well, especially with lighter reds such as ripe Pinot Noir. The question is whether you want more red wine at dessert stage.

Wines with ices were always considered pointless because the coldness of a frozen dessert numbs the taste-buds and strips any good dessert wines of their complexities. This is still the case, but to look at the wave of revisionism that has taken place in this context, you might be forgiven for thinking that ice-cream had suddenly got warmer. Asti! cries one guide, while another warns that sparkling wines clash with the creaminess of ice-cream, before going on to ring the changes from fortified Orange Muscat, fortified southern French Muscat, fine marsala (for chocolate ice-cream), botrytised Chenin from the Loire, botrytised Riesling from South Africa and botrytised Semillon from Australia. The point about the coldness chilling the tastebuds is here glossed over with the advice to make sure that the wine is well chilled too, perhaps in order to ensure that the palate is comprehensively desensitised to anything. You don't need wine with ice-cream, although many desserts that will go with sweet wines often come with a small scoop as garnish. Pouring PX sherry, the oozing, glutinous gunge of heavily raisined grapes, over a bowl of vanilla ice-cream is nice enough for those with an exceptionally sweet tooth, but ultimately more an acknowledgement that nobody would actually want to drink it by the glass. Australian Liqueur Muscats might serve the same function, but by now we have rather wandered out of the realms of food and wine matching, and begun to use the wine itself as an ingredient in the dish.

The whole question of what to drink with desserts is increasingly vexed anyway. A distinguished wine authority once moaned to me over lunch in a City wine bar that the English only let themselves down by drinking dessert wines with desserts. There are those who object to the mere terminology 'dessert wine', saying that it only encourages people to drink them with desserts. As opposed to what? you may wonder, caught in the midst of the appalling vulgarity of opening a bottle of Sauternes to go with the apricot tart. Drink them with blue cheeses, is often the response. The combination of botrytised wine and Roquefort is indeed one of the great juxtapositions. The two kinds of fatty richness go well together, while the intense sweetness of the wine is a perfect counterpoint for the saltiness of the cheese. With other kinds of blue cheese, though, the match is less precise. It isn't great with Stilton or Gorgonzola, and with lighter blues such as Bleu de Bresse, Bleu d'Auvergne or Dolcelatte, it is positively nasty.

The French, to whom one instinctively looks for guidance, are no help at all with sweet wines. They drink them as apéritifs, an unutterably foolish practice. Sweetness is the very last sort of flavour to stimulate the appetite before a meal. Saltiness, sourness, bitterness or dryness all work so well that it seems perverse to opt for the one flavour that doesn't. It has the satiating effect of eating a bar of chocolate between meals, and yet nonetheless, this is what many French do. They have also for generations drunk ruby port as an apéritif, which assaults the palate on two counts – sweetness and tannin. To complete the repertoire of gastronomic incoherence, I was once given a bone-dry, high-acid white wine as an accompaniment to a painfully sweet toffee-based dessert in south-west France. What was the point of this crude collision? Ah, but don't you see, *monsieur*? Just as the sweetness in Sauternes balances the saltiness of Roquefort, so the dryness in this wine balances the sweetness of the dessert! But it didn't. This is not the same analogy at all, but what philosophers call a category error. A counterbalance of sweet and salty is not the same thing at all as a clash between sweet and acidic.

Nonetheless, there is one much-honoured piece of idiocy common to both the British and the French, which is to serve Brut champagne with a dessert. And so we come full circle. Here too, the dryness and acidity of the wine are transformed into a hectoring, spiteful, grimace-inducing nightmare by layers of sugary cream or chocolate or sticky glazes. Presumably, the logic once was that, because a dessert was often the show-stopping course of a dinner, it deserved a suitably grand wine to do it justice. There are sweet champagnes, of course, but hardly anyone sells them now and the dry is thought to be that much more sophisticated. Just like drinking it with eggs, smoked salmon, foie gras, oysters or caviare, so serving dry champagne with desserts is yet another way to ruin it, quite as if it were no more costly than fizzy Lambrusco. It is much better off drunk exactly as it is, as one of the very best appetisers in the world of wine.

If you love wine, you will eat and drink in search of happy matches all the time. Much of the time, you may well drink wine without eating anything at all. It is quite hard for even four people, and virtually impossible for two, to get through a whole bottle of wine in the time it takes to eat the course it has been chosen to accompany. And yet the precise correlation of the one to the other is one of the profoundest pleasures gastronomy can offer. Let the accumulated wisdom of the generations guide you, by all means, but don't let it stifle you and, more important still, feel free to ignore the promulgations of today's gastro-authoritarians. You don't need to know that I ate a smoked quail's egg at Harvey Nichols, and found it went rather nicely with German Riesling. Neither do I, for that matter, which is why I no longer attend such recherché tastings.

Finally, there is one supremely reliable principle that is hardly ever emphasised sufficiently. Quite simply, wherever you are eating a dish that originates in a particular wine-producing region or country, the best wine to drink with it is one from that region or country.

This works at all levels. It is why Alsace whites are so good with foie gras, it is why Côte d'Or burgundy is so splendid with coq au vin, and it is why a basic Italian red is virtually the only thing that goes with pizza. Perhaps the only region in which this doesn't apply is Champagne, where the wine – yet again – proves to be an exception, because it is such an artificial construct. With fusion food, crossover cooking, the new eclecticism, the global larder, call it what you will, the best accompaniments really are the New World wines of Australia, California and South Africa, the places where this experimental style of food originated. Beyond that, the whole subject should be approached in a spirit of speculative curiosity. This is recreation and pleasure, not academic study. Then you can confidently leave the food and wine matching classes to those who found the flower-pressing overbooked.

Chapter 9

SCRAPING THE BARREL

Or: Who are the wine writers and
what do they want?

I N THIS ERA OF VIGOROUSLY increasing worldwide wine consumption, when growing numbers of people seem to know
what they are looking for in the high-street wine merchant's,
and are much less inhibited about expressing both preferences
and antipathies, it comes as something of a jolt to recall the utter
mystification the entire subject once induced in the British.

As little as 30 years ago, anybody keen to expand their wine
horizons might well have seized on a book such as *Make Me A Wine
Connoisseur* by Iain Crawford, one in a series of six-shilling paperbacks that also offered to plug some embarrassing gaps for those
moved to plead *Make Me Understand Pregnancy and Childbirth* or, more
plaintively still, *Make Me A Better Rosegrower*. The blurb promised to
bring enlightenment to the dumbfounded, so that 'ordering at the

vintner's', for example, would no longer be a minefield of potential humiliation, while 'drinking for your own pleasure' would be elevated from the realms of benighted solipsism into a matter of confident illumination.

But you might feel you had been relieved of your six shillings under false pretences as you read on, to be assured that only 'exceptional dedication, an exceptional palate and exceptional opportunities to drink fine wines' could point the way to what the author irresistibly described as the 'bijou residence of connoisseur-manship'. The reader was asked to search his motivations for wanting to know more about wine, and that it was certainly a 'he' the author expected you to be was evidenced by the only half-teasing suggestion that perhaps you wanted '[t]o show off a little to your friends and those doe-eyed young ladies who are always so impressed by vinous knowledge'. After the ritual debunking of the 'foolishly snobbish' types who insist that only certain wines go with certain foods, and a clarion-call for a campaign to demand better provision of half-bottles in restaurants (a plea the annual restaurant guides are still making a generation later), we embark on the opening lessons. Those doe-eyed young ladies of the preamble ensure that we don't quite keep our minds on the subject in hand, for by page 11 the author is in full musk, assuring us that pink wines '[g]o with almost anything but particularly with light dishes without too marked a flavour and candlelit blondes of a suitably young vintage'. One of the most perplexing issues for novices – how to tell whether a wine is faulty – is dispatched with a single line ('If a wine is off, you will notice it at once. It will smell nasty'). A selective geographical tour of the better-known names in each region then follows, and would undoubtedly have given the retentive newcomer a head start in the subject, although there are some curious lacunae. In the section on Bordeaux, for instance, there is no mention of what grape varieties are used in either the red or white wines, information that would now be considered a foundation stone for beginners.

By the end of the book, our worst fears as ingénus are confirmed in a page on wine in restaurants. We are encouraged 'to demand from the wine waiter superb wine, excellent service and the most obsequious flattery at the management's histrionic command', largely on account of the terrible mark-ups charged. The typical wine waiter, we read, turns out to be exactly the cynical, boorish oaf we had always suspected. He should be made to stand and wait while we look at the list, not indulged in his insolence by being allowed to 'bustle' us into choosing, and any attempt by him to suggest a wine or, worse, to jab a finger over our shoulders at an item on the list should be sternly repelled. The trick, presumably, was to spot the finger coming at us from behind and intercept it before it made contact with the page, a manoeuvre for which *Make Me Insuperable In Hand-to-Hand Combat* might offer a useful companion.

The more serious amateur of the period might have availed himself of a much better guide in *Wine*, a weightier fifteen-shilling paperback by one Hugh Johnson, eventually to become Britain's best-selling wine author with his annually updated *Pocket Guide to Wine*. *Wine* was written in the sensuous prose of the true aficionado, blending a narrative approach with its encyclopaedic presentation of the facts, and incorporating some delightfully blurred colour plates. These included a shot of a silver tankard of champagne alongside a dish of caviare, into which was stuck (as if in acknowledgement that the uninitiated were bound to get these things wrong) the faux pas of a metal teaspoon. Most importantly, the author appeared to recognise that if you had bought a book on wine because you enjoyed drinking the stuff, there might be more to its appeal if it spoke directly to that passion. Thus, it opens as follows:

> Think, for a moment, of an almost paper-white glass of liquid, just shot through with greeny-gold, just tart on your tongue, full of wild-flower scents and spring-water freshness. And think of a burnt-umber liquid, as smooth as syrup in the glass, as fat as butter to smell and sea-deep with strange flavours. Both are wine.

What was to make Johnson's *Pocket Guide*, first published in 1977, so popular was precisely that it presented the information contained in the earlier *Wine* in shorthand form, without the *legato* rhapsodies, and in a format that could be slipped surreptitiously out of the inside pocket whilst perusing the shelves in Peter Dominic. 'The wine of Meursault,' you might read in *Wine*, 'is remarkable for being very dry and at the same time soft and mellow. It is described by some people as mealy, reminding them of oatmeal, by others as being like hazel-nuts.' In the pocket edition, that has been clipped down to 'rich, savoury, dry but mellow'. These may not have seemed the most ana-logically precise qualifiers, but they made it easier, should the wine merchant engage you in some landmined badinage about your choice, to respond in kind. 'Ah, a devotee of the Genevrières, I see?' 'Oh yes, I like a rich, savoury wine, one that is dry and yet at the same time mellow.' For the idea of wine-buying as an assault course was scarcely less evident here than in Mr Crawford's slender volume.

Reviewing Johnson's *Wine*, the *Daily Mail* promised its readers that, 'This is more than a book. It is a weapon of self-defence against the wine merchant or the wine snob'.

This constant near-paranoid invocation of the malevolence of sommeliers and off-licence managers is very much a feature of the time, and it was against this tendency that the serious wine writer of the 1960s – of whom Johnson was already identifiably one – wrote his own job specification. Armed with their knowledge, in either the shop or the restaurant, you need not feel disarmed by superior wisdom. Just as those luscious blondes won't look twice at you until you have transformed your physique with the Charles Atlas muscle-pumping kit, so they will consider you a hopeless dork if you simply accept the waiter's wine recommendation in the trattoria, instead of quibbling over the vintage, deploring the mark-up and asking why the establishment does not list the excellent wines of Ischia. As the British middle-classes of the 1960s found themselves able to afford continental holidays, so they often returned with a taste for the local wine of whatever sun-kissed corner of southern Europe they had spent a week in, and wine became the class beverage of the new sophisticates. *Make Me A Wine Connoisseur* might help them bluff their way through. Hugh Johnson's *Wine*, and another concise volume of the period, *Wine Tasting* by auctioneer Michael Broadbent, were for those who meant it.

This, then, was the birth of the modern British wine writer. By the 1980s, broadsheet newspapers would be turning over space to resident wine columnists just as they now catered for motoring, gardening and fashion. Only two obstinate paradoxes attended the investiture of wine-writing as a branch of specialist journalism with general appeal, both of which were implicit in the earliest published efforts of Johnson and Broadbent. One was its over-technicalisation, the very aspect that the pocket editions and how-to manuals were intended to bypass. And the second, for which fault the whole discipline is still ruthlessly pilloried, was all that stuff about butter and hazelnuts and wild flowers. No self-respecting bravo who'd coaxed a candlelit blonde into a bistro was going to compromise his strenuously achieved ascendancy over that bastard wine waiter by suddenly descanting about rose-petals. The whole thing had more than a whiff of poofterism about it, like the wimpy Fotherington-Thomas in the Molesworth books who skips through life apostrophising Nature – 'Hello, trees! Hello, sky!' – instead of designing weaponry. It was to be these factors that, twenty-five years later, would begin to undermine the entire wine-writing enterprise.

What, after all, were these books attempting to do, other than – as the blurbs promised – turn you into precisely the same insufferable snob you had previously resented, by arming you with all his knowledge? Now, when your sister and brother-in-law arrived with a bottle of tissue-wrapped Bourgogne rouge from the off-licence, you could remark before uncorking it, 'Ah, Pinot Noir – that notoriously unreliable grape variety'. To learn about wine, it appeared, the lay enthusiast needed as much information as would be required to pass the Wine and Spirit Education Trust's Higher Certificate, the standard prerequisite for embarking on a serious career in the wine trade. My experience, however, is that people are not especially keen to learn by rote the 1855 classification of Bordeaux, or the *grands crus* of Burgundy. Nor are they particularly fascinated by the chemistry of intracellular fermentation that produces classic

Beaujolais. They are generally interested in knowing about the reputations of recent vintages in the main regions of France, and often want to know what grape variety the wine is based on if it comes from one of the controlled appellations of Europe. They also want to know how to taste, which is why Broadbent's book has never been out of print. But that's about it. Notwithstanding this, many British wine writers, myself included, have produced books for publishers who have asked for a comprehensive entry-level guide to wine, and have felt the need to devote pages to as many of the *denominazioni* and *denominaciones* of the Italian and Spanish wine industries as we can fit in, even though only a tiny proportion of these wines is available in the UK off-trade, and very many are not worth drinking anyway. As the books become more specialised, so the potential readership dwindles to a trainspottery remnant.

Consequently, the newspapers have realised that they don't need an article every Saturday or Sunday profiling the innovative viticultural regime of some Rhône *vigneron* or speculating about the latest quality initiative among the growers of the Rheingau. In a number of the broadsheet papers the editorial space given over to wine is shrinking visibly. And where wine does continue to fill the same amount of space, 'all they want,' a magazine editor told me on behalf of her readers, 'is to be told what to buy and where to buy it.' Not, let it be noted, *why* you think they ought to be buying it. Just shopping lists. Denied even the basic dignity of a descriptive sentence, I resigned from my slot on that magazine.

Then again, it is that descriptive sentence that is often seen as the bone of contention. Ever since Jilly Goolden got an unexpected laugh from the BBC's *Food and Drink* camera team by squeaking out,

'Absolute mangoes!' in the course of nosing a particularly captivating German Riesling, the infamous winespeak has been a matter for public scepticism and hilarity in roughly equal measure. The audience at a public tasting is often quite interested to be told a little of the background to a particular wine, but visibly glazes over as soon as the speaker (and I have been as guilty as anyone) begins asking, 'Do you get blackberries on that? And perhaps a bit of liquorice?' This is now officially known as 'doing a Jilly'. It isn't that such aromas and flavours never exist in wine – but simply that these sense impressions are so subjective that inviting others to agree with you is a doomed enterprise. The mystification implicit in it is consolidated when a speaker rejects a suggestion from the audience – tinned sardines, shoe polish – as inappropriate to describe the nose on a delicate little Vouvray. So it turns out not to be quite so subjective after all. Large numbers of people think winespeak is tedious flannel, and all those speakers and writers who utter it are, quite frankly, too far up their own arses.

One response to the general alienation caused by winespeak is to resort to evaluations of wine relying not on taste descriptors, but on clownish personifications. In this, the *Guardian*'s Malcolm Gluck is the unacknowledged legislator. A wine might thus be said to be a bit of *a gruff old bruiser*, though with *a sentimental streak in there somewhere*. In Gluck's column of 15 January, 2000, he assured us that a German Riesling contained 'nothing Gothic or gimmicky', a saving grace for which it was awarded 15½ points out of 20. At the end, special praise was reserved for a 16-point South African Chardonnay whose nuttiness has an attractive Italian fish-food feel to it. This wine offers brilliance without vulgarity and quietness without being dull –

as one of Proust's railway passengers remarked of a noblewoman with
similar characteristics, is this not the essence of real style?

Here, it might be thought, we are well on the way back here to the
'cheeky little wine of amusing presumption' of blessed satirical
memory. The extraordinary thing is that Gluck is one of those writers who sees himself as being in the vanguard of vanquishing wine
pretension on behalf of the befuddled consumer, and yet here we are
supposed to understand what is meant by describing wines as
'Gothic' or 'quiet', as well as being open to the odd invocation of
Proust.

To these communication problems is added the distressing fact
that there are too many wine writers. Membership of the professional confraternity, the Circle of Wine Writers, which accounts for
by no means all of those attempting to make a living in this field, has,
at the time of writing, just topped 200. Most have no visible national
outlets for their offerings, but scrape what they can writing for tiny
business publications nobody will ever see. When a plum vacancy
arises, the stampede is reminiscent of the opening day of Harrod's
sale. Since there isn't work enough to go around, many members
have turned to other disciplines for supplementary income. Some do
PR work for the trade fronts representing the various foreign wine
industries in the UK. Many have their own commercial interests in
the British wine trade or, in some circumstances, in overseas wine
estates. Still more accept work writing advertising copy under the
pseudo-dignified guise of the greatest con-trick of modern magazine
publishing, advertorial.

Advertorial is not, as its name might imply, a sort of halfway house between a magazine's normal editorial space and advertising. It is advertising pure and simple. Then again, as Mae West might have said, purity has nothing to do with it. It is advertising dressed up to look like a regular feature, only identifiable to the attentive by a small strapline at the top reading 'Advertising Promotion' or 'Promotional Feature'. The intention is to fool the reader into thinking that this colourful double-page spread on the wines of Marsala, for example, has been independently commissioned by the editor. In practice, the editor will have had no choice in the matter, but will have been instructed by the publishers to accept a certain number of fixed advertorial pages each month. Advertorial is considerably more lucrative to the publishers than straightforward, honest-to-goodness advertising for the simple reason that it appears on the page to be what the advertisers crave most of all, i.e. unsolicited third-party endorsement, and they can therefore charge more money for it. As the publisher, you have agreed to make the advertiser's copy look like an innocent article. Some writers only accept these assignments if the copy appears strictly anonymously, but what the advertisers really want are names, and even pictured bylines, and increasingly, this is what they get. Thus are the opinions of supposedly independent commentators bought with a quick phone call and an offer of more cash than they can get for writing editorial copy in the same magazines.

Like Shakespeare's Richard III, they are now in so far in blood, that sin will pluck on sin, and so some then take the next logical step and agree to write endorsement copy in the promotional literature of the retail chains. To have the face of a newspaper wine correspondent beaming lubriciously from the first page of a glossy price-list is thought to convey some higher authority on the document than is derived from peppering it with press quotations that are truly independent. Similarly, most of the big supermarket chains now have an in-house, supposedly general-interest magazine of their own, published under contract for them and always containing a wine section. Thus, for many years, did Malcolm Gluck write a monthly column in *Sainsbury's Magazine* in which, not entirely coincidentally, he heartily recommended scores of Sainsbury's wines each year while Sainsbury's were paying him to do so. Others have followed suit, and the ethical questions screaming to be addressed in these arrangements are presumably never raised. At least, not by those who choose to take the corporate shilling.

Some, no doubt including Malcolm Gluck, justify their involvement in advertorial and retail promotion by claiming that they only accept these agreements when the product is something they have a positive opinion of anyway. In other words, they wouldn't lie. This certainly distinguishes them from those who are happy to lie, enthusiastically endorsing anything if the price is right, but it is nonetheless missing the point. There is such a thing as a conflict of interest, and that some wine writers continue to accept corporate largesse because it is more bounteous than the publishers can afford to pay muddies the waters of public perception for those struggling to remain genuinely unbiased and unbuyable. Appearing at the BBC Good Food exhibition at the NEC one year to talk about a selection of wines, I was asked by one cheerfully blunt member of the audience afterwards how much the winemakers were paying me to say nice things about their products. In the scale of perceived professional probity, it would seem, we are probably on a par with politicians – a shade more credible, at a pinch, than estate agents, but a little less so than used car dealers.

One institution above all is held to provide the most mutually satisfying encounter between the wine trade and those charged with writing about it: the press trip. The PR industry that organises such trips has grown as exponentially over the last twenty years as political consultancy. It is founded on the assumption that tasting wines in a London hotel, whether in the presence of the winemakers or not, is no substitute for tasting them in the regions where they were made.

This is not in itself an unreasonable idea. You do gain a fuller understanding of why Chilean Cabernet Sauvignon is so much richer and riper than its French counterparts if you are standing in the swelter of a Chilean December rather than jostling among the wine industry hoi-polloi at a huge trade tasting in the grizzle of a London October. The conversation you can have with the winemakers is more interactive and enlightening, and it's possible (depending on what stage of the vineyard cycle your visit coincides with) to see how they have trained and pruned their vines, what temperature they are fermenting their wines at, and in what conditions the barrel maturation may take place.

It's also possible – and this is the really enlightening part – to eat, drink and luxuriate at somebody else's expense for anything up to a fortnight. So irresistible does this temptation prove that there are wine writers who devote considerable energy to lobbying the PR companies and trade associations each year to organise trips for them, possibly on the time-hallowed principle that if you don't ask, you won't get. 'My knowledge of what's going on in the San Filippo valley is beginning to look a little patchy. Are you thinking of running a trip in the near future?' Sometimes it even works.

I was once told by a writer trembling reluctantly on the brink of retirement that, in the old days (which may have been as recent as the 1970s), press trips did not have today's wafer-thin patina of spurious ethics. They were cheerfully acknowledged as what they largely are, which is bribes. A minibus full of hacks would be delivered to a reputable château, and the back hatch left unlocked. While they were stumbling through the gloom of the cellars, emitting awestruck gasps from time to time at the dust-coated venerability of it all, or perhaps scoffing down the foie gras at a rather splendid lunch, the minibus would be loaded up with cases of the estate's wine. Nobody would breathe a word about it; to have thanked the hosts would have been to acknowledge the excruciating obviousness of the kickback. It would be divvied up at the airport later, and the quid pro quo would appear in around six months' time in the form of a small item in the *Hereford Bugle* about the unrivalled magnificence of the wines of Château Gratuit.

Time has refined this process to some extent, but not by much. The château now offers you a presentation box or bag, generally of one or two bottles (though sometimes an embarrassing half-dozen), and looks you firmly in the eye. *'Merci de votre visite.' 'Et merci bien de la dégustation.'* For a while, I tried gently refusing these freebies, saying that I had a policy of not accepting gifts as opposed to tasting samples, but the appalling offence often occasioned was more than my mother's-milk British courtesy could stand.

Over the course of a trip lasting several days, and involving half-a-dozen journalists visiting perhaps ten producers, the accumulation of freebies tests the suspension on the Renault Espace to the uttermost. Often, you're not staying in the same hotel for more than one or two nights at a time, so the proliferating bottles are constantly being loaded and unloaded in a Sisyphean labour of dedication. Experience has now taught me ruthlessly to sort through them before each check-out, donating everything between mediocrity and crap to the housekeeping staff, and retaining one or two of the better ones. Others, though – often people advanced in years and wanting in breath at the best of times – are seen determinedly struggling like pack-animals with every last box and bag, as if stockpiling for Christmases to come. Very often, the producers will invite you to choose bottles of your favourite wines to take away, and then, after a little abashed procrastination, one asks for a bottle of the second most valuable wine on offer, with perhaps one of the dankly vegetal rosé as well so as not to appear to have succumbed exclusively to unseemly greed.

There are producers now who do not offer freebies, at least not bottles, but merely shake one's hand and smile politely. This is increasingly the case in Champagne, to the chagrin of many, but when a producer of rather good Spanish cava rounded off a visit by ceremoniously presenting each journalist with a repulsive ceramic pot containing a bag of toffees, the disappointment was tangible. An apron for the kitchen, a wall calendar, cod diplomas with my name calligraphed in to denote my induction to some metaphorical confraternity, hardback souvenir picture-books, a crystal glass stencilled with my initials bemusingly rendered as 'St W' as though I had been elevated to the company of saints – all these have come my way, and more, although the cuddly toy has so far eluded me.

In the dear old days, press trips were offered and accepted without condition, the assumption being that if the findings warranted press exposure, a place would be found for them at some unspecified later date – perhaps as much as a year later. The occupational uncertainty that is the lot of most freelance wine writers, together with a more hawkishly aggressive PR industry, has inevitably consigned such genteel understandings to the dustbin of history. These days, the expectation is that if a trip is offered, you will schedule it for your weekly column on a promised date. If you don't have a weekly column, you will be expected to contact the specialist press, such as *WINE* magazine, *Decanter* or one of the gastronomic magazines to see if you can place a feature, and thus claim your Business Class seat. Foreign wine producers often don't understand the extent to which wine-writing in the UK press is a contracted-out activity, and so the PRs are under pressure to attach a publication title to each name rather than send you out under the queasily nebulous designation 'Freelance'. This often results in two freelances turning up on the same trip apparently from the same magazine, as though one were tasting the wines and the other holding the spit-bucket.

In one sense, the requirement for a prior commission may be thought good commercial discipline, weeding out the more conspicuous freeloaders before the plane leaves the tarmac. On the other hand, it isn't hard to feel – as you frantically ring round the editorial desks trying to win authorisation for a week in southern Italy – as though you are acting merely as a compliant arm of the PR industry. And then again, with freelances generally about as welcome in some regions as an outbreak of black rot, there is an absurd bias in favour of taking anybody who happens to be on staff somewhere, whatever their background, specialisation or likelihood of writing up the trip.

These non-specialists, who may be newshounds, fashion correspondents, even junior sub-editors, are the Typhoid Marys of wine press trips. Incapable of absorbing any of the information themselves, all too often they undermine the proceedings even for the properly qualified. They thought they were in for a treat, one long piss-up interspersed with blow-out dinners at Michelin-starred restaurants, and can't understand why, once they have seen one lot of fermentation tanks, they should be expected to look at nine more. Grumbling loudly, they invent sudden ailments to get out of the itinerary at least until lunchtime ('I might be able to manage a *little* filet mignon now'). For many, the trip has been handed to them as a lollipop for working a lot of overtime or not asking for a rise, and this feels just too much like hard work. On one trip, a tabloid reporter inquired quizzically in the cellars at Krug champagne why many of the older bottles were so thick with dust, perhaps imagining the charlady needed a bit of a ticking-off. On another, a Royal reporter from one of the Sundays had the deeply awkward misfortune to be stuck on a ten-day wine trip in Chile when the news of Charles and Diana's separation was announced, and spent long nights phoning through copy from his hotel-room, sleeping off his exertions during the day while the rest of us toured the vineyards.

The reward for all the exertions, all the tastings, all the weary tramping through the vinescapes of the Languedoc, the Rhineland and La Mancha is scant indeed. Unless you are writing for one of the newspapers, the rates of pay are generally pitiful. The specialist wine monthlies, for all that they are stuffed with advertorial, pay their staff and freelance contributors very little. Royalties from a book on the wines of southern Portugal are not expected to make anybody a living.

The other form of inducement seen as more dignified is wine-writing awards. These are now legion, and naturally all sponsored by drinks manufacturers, national trade fronts or wine merchants. Everyone loves an awards ceremony, and there is a burgeoning sense these days, as the competitions open to wine writing proliferate that, as under the rules of the Caucus-race in *Alice's Adventures in Wonderland*, 'all have won, so all must have prizes'. The motivation for offering the free study trips, cases of slosh and occasional cash prizes that come with these accolades is allegedly to acknowledge journalistic excellence, and yet one suspects the mechanics of them are much more to do with encouraging wine writers to seek commissions to write favourable copy about the wines in question.

At the top of the tree are the Glenfiddich Awards, an annual gongfest for food and drink writers paid for by William Grant and Sons, makers of the eponymous single-malt whisky. The Glenfiddichs have been running for nearly thirty years now, and are taken very seriously by the publishing industry as well as by those who have spent half a day photocopying their magazine articles for the scrutiny of the judges. Over the years the Glenfiddich awards have become as ethically watertight as it is probably possible for awards to get. But sometimes the impression is given of uneasy conflicts of interest. In 1996, for example, Allan Cheesman of Sainsbury's wine department sat on the panel as the wine specialist. In the category of Drink Writer of the Year, the shortlist of two (half the usual number) comprised Malcolm Gluck, then wine writer of *Sainsbury's Magazine*, and Jancis Robinson, whose television production company had received a subvention towards her latest BBC wine series from J. Sainsbury plc. There is no suggestion that anyone had acted improperly in any way, but the judging chairman, a scion of the Grant family, later insisted he couldn't see anything untoward in a panel on which the only wine specialist was an employee of J. Sainsbury plc.

Fortunately, we don't have to rely on William Grant and Sons or Sainsbury's to identify good wine writing for us. It is there for those who care to look, although the weekly wine columns are not any longer its best repository. Perhaps surprisingly, the most prominent names in the business really are the better writers. Hugh Johnson's body of work – in particular, the majestic historical sweep of his 1989 *The Story of Wine* – is a towering achievement, and while it certainly has an element of the patrician about it, manages not to alienate the non-specialist reader. It is a friendly, even slightly avuncular voice, the sonorous tone of the amiable old gent telling grand stories by the fireside after dinner. Jancis Robinson has the gift of talking descriptively about wine without ever veering into pretentiousness. She seems to know what will and won't wash with a sceptical public, and her ability to explain quite complex technical procedures in a straightforward, uncluttered fashion is worth cherishing. Perhaps more than anyone else currently working, she has contributed vastly to the accumulated store of wine knowledge with her meticulously researched work on grape varieties, as well as the periodically updated *Oxford Companion to Wine*, of which she is editor. And for all his relentlessly demotic rough-and-readiness, and tendency to spread himself exceeding thin, there is no better introductory writer than Oz Clarke. You may not agree with half of his opinions, but at least he has opinions, and is more than happy to express them with galvanising force. Among the dear departed, John Arlott – as authoritative on wine as he was on cricket – and Cyril Ray – bon vivant, socialist, editor of the annual *Compleat Imbiber* and founder of the Circle of Wine Writers – are the authentic voices of an earlier era. This may have been a time when the British were cowering before the might of the supercilious sommelier, but Ray's work in particular helped to liberate wine from the shackles of class-based exclusivity.

Outside the specialist writers, the next best source of good wine writing lies in the gastronomic field. Notoriously in Britain, as distinct from continental Europe, food and wine writing are not seen as occupying the same planet. Cookery writers haven't the faintest idea what wines to recommend with their recipes (and I should have forfeited a considerable amount of income over the years if they did), and most wine writers, despite being formidable eaters, are blissfully ignorant of the principles of cooking. Additionally, membership of the respective professional associations indicates a fairly pronounced gender split. To the wine expert, the cookery writers seem a lot of silly old biddies obsessed with self-raising flour, while the recipe-writers see in the former only a pack of rubicund old buffers united in keeping alive the vibrantly patterned bow-tie.

'Twas emphatically not ever thus. M. F. K. Fisher, possibly the greatest American gastronomic writer of them all, wrote beautifully on wine and other drinks, even though it was by no means her specialist subject. A compendium volume of five of her books, published in 1991 as *The Art of Eating*, is a goldmine of understated, elegant and poignantly evocative writing. She is as good as she is because she realises that even the greatest wealth of technical information, or indeed the most rapturous prose about its flavours, cannot match connecting wine to the real people who drink and serve it. Dining alone in the north of Burgundy in 1936, she orders a bottle of seven-year-old Chablis from an exceedingly solicitous waitress:

> I was fascinated by her method of uncorking a vintage wine. Instead of the Burgundian procedure of infinite and often exaggerated precautions against touching or tipping or jarring the bottle, she handled it quite nonchalantly, and seemed to be careful to keep her hands only from the cool bottle itself, holding it sometimes by the basket and sometimes in a napkin. The cork was very tight, and I thought for a minute that she would break it. So did she; her face grew tense, and did not loosen until she had slowly worked out the cork and dried the lip. Then she poured an inch of wine in a glass, turned her back to me like a priest taking Communion, and drank it down. Finally some was poured for me, and she stood with the bottle in her hand and her full lips drooping until I nodded a satisfied yes.

Recalling the alcohol she was plied with at numerous seduction scenes, *dîners à deux* where she must have bemusedly played the 'candlelit blonde' of Mr Crawford's revved-up imagination, she acknowledges that

> I was given some beautiful liquids: really old Scotch, Swiss Dézelay light as mountain water, proud vintage Burgundies, countless bottles of champagne, all good too, and what fine cognacs! Only once did a professional bachelor ever offer me a glass of sweet liqueur. I never saw him again, feeling that his perceptions were too dull for me to exhaust myself, if after even the short time needed to win my acceptance of his dinner invitation he had not guessed my tastes that far.

Into the gulf that yawns between a fluteful of effervescing Pol Roger and a silly little noggin of Parfait Amour, we watch a possible affair go tumbling.

Another US writer, Jay McInerney, bratpack author of *Bright Lights, Big City* and *Story of My Life*, was given a wine column on American *House & Garden* in 1995, in the spirit – now sweeping British newspaper and periodical publishing – of farming such work out to people who have no visible qualification to undertake it (other than being famous for something unrelated). Whereas in the UK, though, that has meant the widely loathed Michael Winner reviewing restaurants or Dirty Den from *EastEnders* writing about wine, it has in the States been a slightly more imaginative enterprise. What McInerney imparts is very basic wine information, researched no less punctiliously, it would seem, than the self-conscious amateur owes to the general reader, but the prose is fresh, crisp and witty, and the personifications he prefers to the 'buttercups and compost' approach work a whole lot more evocatively than do those of certain so-called specialists in the field in British journalism. 'If Corton-Charlemagne resembles a novel by one of the Brontë sisters,' ventures McInerney, 'then Chablis is an early Raymond Carver story.' Elsewhere, he memorably avers that '[t]he cool, pale beauty of champagne is, like that of Ingrid Bergman and Greta Garbo, the product of a chilly climate'. Nor is he any respecter of sensibilities. Apostrophising a particularly concentrated Australian Shiraz (Clarendon Hills' Astralis) that he considers 'the most extracted, inky, macho red wine I have ever encountered', he advises

> [I]f you've got plenty of cash, durable enamel on your teeth, and the patience to wait fifteen years, I highly recommend it. Eat it with smoked kangaroo or perhaps grilled *Tyrannosaurus rex* steaks rubbed with chilli.

No mention of American wine writers can be considered comprehensive without some reference to Robert Parker, often thought to be the most powerful wine commentator on the planet. His judgments, pronounced with stentorian authority in his journal *The Wine Advocate* and in his regularly updated book *The Wine Buyer's Guide*, are received as holy writ all over the world. He appears to do nothing other with his life than taste wine, whether on his self-financed trips to Europe, or his travels around the Americas, or at home in his kitchen in Maryland, and the result of this all-consuming obsession is a minutely calibrated marking system where every wine is given a score out of 100. The vagaries of this system are such that a wine scoring in the 70s is a flat disappointment. Eighty-something is getting pretty good, while a wine in the 90s is what all the shouting's about. Such is the influential nature of this approach that, in a famous adage of the US wine trade, if Parker gives a wine higher than 90, you can't get it, and if he gives it lower than 90, you can't sell it. These most considered judgements are certainly hard to ignore. Nobody seriously suggests that Parker is anything other than a highly refined and experienced taster, for all that he is thought to be sounder in some areas (Bordeaux, the Rhône, Piedmont) than in others (Burgundy, Germany and Australia). The price of his opinions is not merely the £40 asked for the latest edition of *The Wine Buyer's Guide*, but a prose style so pedestrian and repetitious, as dense and chewy as one of his beloved northern Rhône reds, that perusal of the tasting notes is a dispiriting task indeed. Everything seems to be full of 'gobs of sweet, jammy fruit' (whatever those might be) or 'huge, opulent, glycerine-laden, spectacular, mind-blowing depth', and the cumulative effect of the writing is an object-lesson in how adjectival pile-ups, far from contributing to our enlightenment, can have a paradoxically dimming effect.

The best literary passages on wine, it has always seemed to me, are not those that try to capture the essence of a particular taste – once apprehended, never to be regained – but those unabashedly reconnecting wine with the reason we come to it in the first place, which is that it is an alcoholic drink. Ernest Hemingway, a heroic drinker who would – if he were living at this hour – just have been offered a wine column on *Beautiful Home* magazine, catches this point beautifully in *Death in the Afternoon*:

> I would rather have a palate that would give me the pleasure of enjoying completely a Château Margaux or a Haut-Brion, even though excesses indulged in in the acquiring of it have brought a liver that will not allow me to drink Richebourg, Corton, or Chambertin, than to have the corrugated iron internals of my boyhood when all red wines

were bitter except port and drinking was the process of getting down enough of anything to make you feel reckless.

More than anything else, and with Hemingway's ruminations in mind, it is necessary for wine writing to resist the incursions of the sensible-drinking mafia, if it is to have even a fraction of the cheering effect on the soul the stuff itself does. This is a theme on which I have myself written at length elsewhere, and which it is scarcely possible to articulate any longer without inviting a deluge of sanctimonious opprobrium. Wine's power to console the heart and insulate the spirits was established in humanity's infancy, is celebrated in the work of most of the writers I have been discussing here, from M. F. K. Fisher to Jancis Robinson, but is under attack as never before from the combined forces of a hostile medical profession and a mood of neo-Prohibitionism that is rampant in America and may well be on its way here. In leaner, hungrier times, the truth can more easily be told, as it was only half-ironically in the Foreword to the *Savoy Cocktail Book* of 1930:

In moments of stress and strain wine is man's greatest friend. Once, many years ago, a great and good man, somewhat my senior in age, made a very shrewd and important observation to me. We had been discussing the misfortunes of a mutual friend who had been working so hard that he had forced himself into a state of brain-fever: a salient point in the case was that he imagined he could keep his brain clearer by eating and drinking extremely little, whereas this abstemiousness on his part had only succeeded in hastening his collapse

'My boy,' said my friend to me, 'Let this be a solemn lesson to us all to eat as much good food, and drink as much good wine, as we possibly can, when and wherever the opportunity presents itself, no matter what it costs – or who pays for it.'

It is this last philosophical point that matters more about wine, in the final reckoning, than whether the 1996 was a better vintage than the '97 in Nuits-St-Georges, or what precisely it tasted like, or how much you could expect to get for it in a few years' time if you bought a case for laying down, or whether it would be better drunk with partridge or with grouse. But hardly anybody is now prepared to say so.

Can the ethical swamp that wine writing has become ever be cleaned up? The answer is probably no, and the chances will decrease in inverse proportion to the slice of the alcohol retail sector that wine accounts for. The more popular the stuff, the more people will be trying to get in on the act. Who wouldn't want monthly deliveries of unsolicited wine samples from PR companies and retailers arriving at the door?

The Circle of Wine Writers runs an entertaining column in its journal, in which sightings of freeloaders at trade and press tastings are reported. They have usually invited themselves, and often give the names of bogus publications for which they are supposedly the wine contributors. Having lied their way in, they can easily be spotted by their behaviour. Some are there for nothing more than the free lunch generally offered, and are sure to avail themselves of seconds wherever they can. Others don't neglect to drink their fill from the opened bottles. In an environment of small sips and genteel spitting, it takes some nerve to be seen slugging back a whole glass of classed-growth claret, growing ever unsteadier on your feet as you totter round from table to table. Only one thing bothers me about the Circle's merciless ragging of such impostors. The rankly inebriated we may safely despise, but how do we know, in the case of the 'wine columnist' from the *East Chiltington Enquirer* nervously dribbling Puligny-Montrachet into the sawdust, that we won't be electing him to the committee next year?

Chapter 10

READING THE WINE LEES

Things can only get better – or can they?

F I HAVE PAINTED A rather sombre picture of what happened to wine during the course of the 1990s, it ought – you might think – to be incumbent on my concluding chapter to present some more hopeful pointers to the future. Conventional wisdom has it that it is easier to be critical than to offer considered approval, and indeed there is a strand of thought within wine-writing circles that would prefer just to remain silent about sloppy wine-making practices – all the corner-cutting, cheating and adulteration that goes on – in the interests of emphasising the positive aspects. This attitude gives me nightmares. Nothing will ever improve for the consumer if those in a position to hold the miscreants and the under-achievers to account assiduously decline to do so.

To a certain sort of old-school wine writer, the benefits of what they imagine to be a profession, that come in the form of monthly deliveries of free wine from the supermarket chains and trips to sun-soaked vinescapes in both hemispheres, represent a boat not worth rocking by making negative evaluations. Within what I see as the duty to tell the truth as I find it, there are certainly niceties of judgement. Sometimes a visit to a struggling small wine producer is the occasion for sadness, because the best they are undoubtedly doing will never be good enough to compete. You express your opinion, and then draw a line through your notes. Then again, the visit to a major conglomerate with hundreds of hectares of vineyard land, up-to-the-minute lab technology, restaurant and accommodation facilities, a very handsome PR budget . . . and shatteringly dull, mainstream wines, is a sharper spur to criticism because they already command a larger market share than they deserve. In the latter case, anyway, a certain quotient of criticism can be happily soaked up, whereas the smaller producer may be hyper-sensitive to the faintest suggestion of being caught out. In a Languedoc winery one year, I enquired innocently enough about the typical fermentation temperatures for a batch of red wines that tasted cooked and muddy. The *vigneron*'s paroxysm of fury, throwing his glass down and stalking off among the fermentation vats, suggested that he knew I knew, indeed we all knew, a nail had been hit on the head. (When he could be coaxed to return, he spluttered out something about wine being made in the vineyard and in the cellar and not in an office, not a statement one would quibble with, but no excuse for his hideous, stewed wines.)

The ethics of wine writing get murkier by the year. This will not improve. Not only are more and more people getting into the racket, but there is also less and less meaningful work for them. What is technically known as a heated debate on this subject took place in the Circle of Wine Writers in the summer of 2000. Some of those members regularly accepting money for sponsored work, whether for writing in supermarket magazines, PR consultancy, advertorial or even producing corporate monographs on a particular wine producer (*Lust for Perfection: The Story of Louis Zob*), appeared sincerely to have convinced themselves that their strings were not in any way being pulled by these paymasters. In the case of advertorial, the magazine reader can see perfectly well by the byline who is paying the hired monkey. So too with some other paid endorsements. But that is not always the case and it is misleading to dress up paid-for views as pieces of independent journalism. As a result, wine writing as a branch of serious journalism is almost dead.

If the wine writers can safely be ignored, then most wine consumers will be left with what the high-street retailers choose to sell them. It is already difficult enough to warn people away from the 40% of wines on sale rejected as unfit each year by the International Wine Challenge, because all the newspapers and magazines want to print are rave reviews. When even the shopping lists of recommendations in the wine columns are not to be trusted, though, because you don't know if the writer is being paid to say them and if so, by whom, consumers will have to arrive at their own more or less informed judgements. It is hard, in this light, to see the loss of adventurousness in the high-street wine trade that I regretted in chapter 1 easily being made good. There is no sound financial reason for the multiples to undermine the trading relationships they enjoy with their regular suppliers if they can persuade them to keep sup-plying more of the same old varietal wines that have kept the market so docile. Trailing the global winemaking consultant about like packs of salivating beagles after a fox, they have discovered what a breeze wine retailing can be if you just don't exert yourself with too many small-scale contracts. Eventually, however, the nature of a market does change, often for quite unfathomable reasons. Maybe, you may conclude one day, varietal Merlot isn't such an unalloyed blessing, as you sip at another brittle, bitter vin de pays d'Oc. Perhaps Sauvignon Blanc that doesn't really taste of anything is traducing the name of that variety, so you mistakenly stop buying the ones that are still full of aromatic personality. Perhaps Viognier, in recent years the great white hope to supplant Chardonnay for when we're all sick to the back palate of that grape, will seem a pointless variety to those who have only tasted thin Languedoc versions or the California example that tastes of honey-and-lemon throat sweets. Developments like these could well throw the beagles off the scent, and force them to start exploring some of the forgotten byways once again, but I have to confess I sense a whole lot more mileage in the present formula.

There will continue to be a growing number of wines appearing from the most unlikely areas at extraordinarily preposterous prices, particularly from the independent wine merchants. Every up-and-coming wine region now wants its own handful of super-cuvées, wines for which £25 is demanded in the naïve hope that the price alone will persuade you that this must be the new Sassicaia, even the new Château Latour. These are truly the doomed wines of the pres-ent generation. Sheer novelty (as well as undoubted quality) helped to create a regular niche market for the likes of Tuscany's Sassicaia or

California's Opus One in an era when such things were all but unheard-of. Indisputably, these wines helped to raise the profile of regions the old guard of wine critics would simply not have considered in the same class as the old French heartlands. But the trend has become a cynical, and – if its exponents would but see it – ultimately self-defeating, exercise now that more and more of them are being launched. On balance, and quite unscientifically, I would argue that one can be more confident these days that spending more money will guarantee a correspondingly better bottle, but it will never by definition be the golden rule, not least because such judgements are always so woefully, but also gloriously, subjective. And also because there is still, as the Challenge tasters annually remind us, a hell of a lot of godawful wine out there, by no means all of it the cheapest of the cheap.

As to the under-performing classics, I think we can allow ourselves a cautious squeak of optimism. The days when you could sell whatever garbage you turned out, simply because it was entitled to call itself Chianti or Bordeaux, are long behind us. There is still garbage about, of course, and for some reason a number of our high-street buyers keep on buying it, but as others have gone in search of better wines in areas where there is no shortage of people making wine, so the laggards have been forced to smarten up their acts. Many of these producers may be happy to go back to selling locally, in which case we scarcely need to worry about them, but most would give their eye-teeth (or trade the odd bag of sulphur dioxide) to secure or retain an export contract, and here the British buyers can award themselves a little credit for modestly raising the overall quality. If you must have Chianti – and you won't suffer a dangerous dietary lack if you don't – the chances that it will be drinkable slosh, as opposed to repellent swill, are somewhat improved.

The influence of the flying winemakers can, sadly, only grow. As more and more power is vested in them by the retailers, they will wield greater and greater economic clout, and be able to extend themselves into areas where there isn't yet a great deal of export activity. It is a source of regret that when a relatively new wine region appears on our market, it is nearly always under the imprimatur of one of the international consultants. Some of these have, nobly enough, tried to work with indigenous varieties. Peter Bright makes Chardonnays and Cabernets by the tanker-load, but he also makes such wines as Baga and Trincadeira in Portugal and Negroamaro in Italy, seeking to preserve some of the regional style instead of subsuming it under a one-size-fits-all philosophy of homogenisation. The generality, though, is dull, predictable wines, made in some cases to recipes stipulated by the retail buyers themselves, and advertised as such at the press tastings and on the labels: 'We asked Brad Tipple MW to make us a Chardonnay to suit modern tastes at this newly established Romanian winery, and we are delighted with the results. This buttery, peachy wine, which would be ideal with chicken, fish, meats, salads, pasta, quiche, vegetarian foods, kebabs, burgers, SuperNoodles and chewing-gum, is enriched by subtle oaky flavours and would be ideal drunk within ten minutes of purchase. Enjoy in moderation.'

As to the question of oak, we are of course stuck with it, and it shouldn't be forgotten that without it winemaking would be pitifully impoverished. We might wish that oak flavour wasn't sprayed on to quite so many wines to lend them some spurious, extraneous personality, but I would still wager that anybody's Top Ten list of their favourite wines ever would consist overwhelmingly of wines that have had some wood treatment. If winemakers feel that their wines lack personality without it, perhaps that is to some extent because they are all so deeply in hock to Chardonnay, a grape that doesn't possess a great deal of intrinsic character of its own, especially in the warmer climates. Planting some more aromatic varieties might do the trick, and would save on the fretful expense of barrels – or even those bags of chips they are all so embarrassed about using. Then again, if the Chardonnay'n'chips formula is working for them commercially, who are they to worry about drab standardisation?

Champagne will go on entrancing and infuriating us in roughly equal proportion. Short of another biting recession, it seems unlikely that the British wine trade will ever be able to secure us a fair deal on price, and so we shall continue to be milked for all we are worth if that is the fizz we want to drink. At least the quality is up on what we were getting at the end of the 1980s. The regional Quality Charter improved matters immensely, and even though the wine of some fairly dreadful years had to go into the non-vintage blends in the early 1990s, the picture in the latter half of the decade – that is, the wines we are drinking now – is considerably brighter. One single initiative that would transform the buying of champagne for the good in this country would be if the buyers found time to visit a few of the many small growers in the region, and featured some of their wines alongside the famous names. Waitrose bought some sound wine from an organic grower called

Fleury in 1999, and were able to sell it at a price that undercut everything but their own-brand range. It was rich and appetising stuff, a little rustic maybe compared to Moët et Chandon, but then champagne is the one wine that might benefit from a little rusticity. As to other dry sparkling wines, they will continue at their best to fulfil the role expected of them, which is as more cost-effective substitutes for champagne that may occasionally attain to something like the complexity and depth of the original.

The treatment of wine in restaurants can still realistically be improved, but it depends, crucially, on customers speaking up about high-handed practices and boycotting places with disgracefully expensive lists. Not buying wine at over-inflated prices may seem like a decision that most of us would make perforce anyway, but actually we are all colluding in rapacious profiteering whenever we pay £5 for a single glass or £20 for a bottle of *vin de pays*. Actively support those restaurants that are demonstrably offering a fair deal on wine (assuming the cooking is good too), and make a point of telling those that aren't – in writing afterwards if you're shy about speaking up – that your enjoyment of your evening out with them was undermined by the embarrassing greed of their mark-up policy. If you only want a glass, inquire as to the size of the measure. If it is less than 175ml, ask why. Tell them not to keep topping you up, send back all out-of-condition bottles without demur, and if you do drink sherry, ask first whether the bottle has been chilled and ruthlessly reject every last tot of stale fino.

The matching of food and wine is a burgeoning specialism. To some journalists it is the last redoubt now that the commissioning editors won't take in-depth analysis or interviews with winemakers.

It has now expanded from a *de rigueur* section in the comprehensive introductory wine guides to whole books. Among all the baleful tendencies anatomised in this book, however, this one need give you the least concern. It is perfectly easy to ignore. Work out your own preferred combinations instead of taking their word for it, but for goodness' sake, don't stick to them. Try out new ones all the time. And feel free to disregard the received wisdoms. Virtually the entire wine writing profession believes, following French practice, that botrytised sweet wines such as Sauternes are the *ne plus ultra* with foie gras. You may not yet have discovered within yourself a burning desire to determine what wine is best to drink with foie gras, but it sure as hell isn't Sauternes. It results in a repulsive mismatch, the richly fatty density of the food (especially in a pâté or terrine) creating a mouth-coating sensation of true horror when added to the syrupy texture of a sweet wine. It is not just cloying, it is almost sick-making, and one must only conclude that those who indulge themselves in this way are doing it for no better reason than to consume two outrageously expensive things at once. Reject any book that advises this match. It can only be the work of an overgrown infant.

It is a truth universally acknowledged that all judgements in matters of food and drink are subjective through and through. Indeed, it would be a washed-out world if things were any different. What you have been reading are nothing but my own considered opinions on matters that affect today's wine world, but tend not to be aired very often in the specialist wine magazines. But because they are matters that affect the flavour, the quality and the price of what you drink, I have thought it worthwhile to bring them to your attention. Informed consumers are empowered consumers, which is what we all should be. And I guarantee that no wine company or wine producer has paid or will pay me for my opinions. An informed consumer deserves nothing less.

index